# Soul time

# Soul time

## BUILDING A

## RELATIONSHIP

## WITH GOD

Peter Atkins

St. Louis, Missouri

© Copyright 1999 by Peter Atkins

All rights reserved. No part of this book may be reproduced without written permission from Chalice Press, P.O. Box 179, St. Louis, MO 63166-0179.

Bible quotations, unless otherwise noted, are from the *New Revised Standard Version Bible*, copyright 1989, Division of Christian Education of the National Council of the Churches of Christ in the United States of America. Used by permission. All rights reserved.

Scripture quotations marked (TEV) are taken from the *Today's English Version*—Second Edition ©1992 by American Bible Society. Used by permission.

Extracts from *A New Zealand Prayer Book*, © 1989, Collins, London are used with permission.

Cover design: Lynne Condellone
Cover photo: "Solo" © Gregory Lawler, Small Planet Photography, 1997
Interior design: Elizabeth Wright
Art Director: Elizabeth Wright

This book is printed on acid-free, recycled paper.

Visit Chalice Press on the World Wide Web at
www.chalicepress.com

10 9 8 7 6 5 4 3 2 1         99 00 01 02 03

**Library of Congress Cataloging–in–Publication Data**

Atkins, Peter, Rev.
   Soul Time : building a relationship with God / Peter Atkins.
      p.   cm.
   Includes bibliographical references and index.
   ISBN 0-8272-3445-7
   1. Spiritual life—Christianity.  I. Title.
BV5401.2 .A834   1999
248.4—dc21
                                                   99–050440
                                                         CIP

Printed in the United States of America

*This book is dedicated to those students in preparation for ministry who trusted me enough to ask for guidance and support during their spiritual pilgrimages.*

# Contents

| | |
|---|---|
| Acknowledgments | ix |
| Introduction | 1 |
| 1. Awareness of the Presence of God | 5 |
| 2. Relating to the God of the Scriptures | 19 |
| 3. Dealing with Our Fears | 33 |
| 4. Worship and Affirmation | 49 |
| 5. Widening the Concepts of God and Ourselves | 63 |
| 6. Coping with the Storms in Life | 77 |
| 7. Intercession and Healing | 91 |
| 8. Cultural and Gendered Views of God | 105 |
| 9. Sin and Forgiveness | 119 |
| 10. Thanksgiving | 133 |
| 11. The Withdrawal of God | 147 |
| 12. Using a Spiritual Director | 161 |
| Conclusion | 173 |
| Bibliography | 175 |
| Index | 177 |

# Acknowledgments

I am grateful to the Reverend Frank Hanson, a friend and colleague in the Auckland Consortium for Theological Education, who read the manuscript and offered most useful comments; to Dr. Jon L. Berquist, academic editor at Chalice Press; and as always to my wife, Rosemary, for her patience, support, and encouragement. I am also grateful to Mr. Robin Nairn, the general secretary of the Anglican Church in Aotearoa, New Zealand, and Polynesia on behalf of its General Synod for permission to use certain passages as noted in the references from its prayer book published by Collins, London, in 1989. In accordance with their request, I record this formal acknowledgment: The copyrighted material on pages 52, 86, 134, 144, 146, 149, and 150 is taken from *A New Zealand Prayer Book: He Karakia Mihinare o Aotearoa*, and is used with permission.

My thanks also to Rigby Publishers of Australia for the use of the poem "Doubts," by Pauline Young, included in *An Anthology of Christian Verse,* edited by Francis Byrne, O.S.B., 1983.

# Introduction

### Enlarging the Spirit, Feeding the Soul

The word *spirituality* is on the lips of many Christians today. We face a materialistic world, and many have reacted to the collapse of faith and the breakdown in relationships in society. In contrast, they are appreciating the spiritual dimension of life. They admire the saints of previous ages, when time for reflection had a higher priority than is given in the busy-ness of today. Such admiration has often turned to study and study to a challenge to spend more of our lives in *soul time,* enlarging the spirit and feeding the soul.

Saint Augustine wrote in his books of *Confessions:*

> You prompt us to honor You, making it a joy to praise You.
> You have created us to relate to you,
> and our hearts are not at rest until they find their rest in You.
> Help me, Lord, to know and accept in my soul
> which comes first:
> to search You out or to praise You,
> to relate to You
>     or to know the name by which to speak with You.
>
> They shall praise the Lord that seek their God.
> They that search for God will find the presence of the Lord.
> And in the presence of the Lord they shall praise their God.[1]

Much later in the same collection, the saint longs for others to share his experiences of God:

> O that people might turn from their occupation with material
>     things,
> and seek You, their true God.
> For though they have abandoned You, their Creator,
> You will not abandon any of Your creatures.
> O that all may turn to You and search You out.
> Behold You are there in their hearts,
> in the hearts of those who trust that You exist.

---

[1] Author's paraphrase of parts of Book I, chapter 1 of the *Confessions.*

> They leap into Your lap
> and weep for the wanderings that have worn them out.
> Your gentle hand wipes away their tears,
> as they weep these are turned to tears of joy.
> For Your power is not weak like our poor mortal power.
> You are God;
> You can renew what You have created
> and grant us consolation.
> When I began to look for You, I thought I would lose touch with myself,
> but there You were in front of me and within me,
> the very person whom I had deserted.
> When I could not find myself,
> how could I find You?
> When I did find You,
> there was (and is) refreshment and true courage.[2]

A more recent master of spiritual development, Carlo Carretto, writes of his own faith in his experiences:

> When anyone asks me, especially after I have come back from the desert,
> "Brother Carlo, do you believe in God?" I answer
> "Yes, I tell you in the Holy Spirit, I do believe."
> And if my questioner's curiosity is aroused to the point of inquiring further,
> "What evidence do you bring forward for asserting so great a truth?"
> I say, to conclude the conversation,
> "Only this: I believe in God because I know him."[3]

Later he says:

> If God exists, I want to know him;
> I want to meet him.
> I want to grow accustomed to being near him.
> I want to contemplate him.
> I want to seek my God with the whole of myself
> and not merely with the proudest part of myself, my reason.[4]

---

[2] Author's paraphrase of the last section of Book V, chapter 2 and the last line of chapter 1 of the *Confessions*.
[3] Carlo Carretto, *I Sought and I Found* (London: Darton, Longman, and Todd, 1984), 21.
[4] Ibid., 59.

## A Primer

Encouraged by the writings of such old and new spiritual giants, I have written this book to put into the hands of many a way to start the journey to maturity. My book does not aim to be a spiritual classic, but a primer for those who are inquiring into how to take the first steps on the journey of spiritual development. It has been born out of the joy of sharing these first steps with a number of students and parishioners over a substantial period of ministry—both as a pastor and as a teacher. Such spiritual growth is enabled by what I have called *soul time*, which is time set aside for our relationship with God. This is in addition to, rather than as a substitution for, our public and private prayer, study of the Bible, and other theological writings. As the Christian faith is both corporate and personal, we must pay attention to our growth in both these aspects. In an age of individualism, Christians are called to stress the corporate relationship to Christ and the church, as well as our intimate personal relationship to God in Trinity.

Too many people have never had an opportunity to structure this personal development and have never dared to take the first steps on a personal journey of growth in their relationship with the Divine. They may attend worship and pick up the scraps of information and inspiration for such a journey but never realize the need to examine it in detail, either by reading such a book as this or by sharing their desire with an experienced soul friend.

This book is a primer in the sense that it begins at the beginning with how we might be aware of the presence of God, and then it takes us through a further eleven chapters that cover in outline the essential stages on such a journey. It is also a primer in the sense that it aims to "prime the pump," allowing the water of spiritual life to flow more freely, and thus getting people started who may be eager to learn but do not know how to begin. Like the primers in every type of education, it sets out to provide the basic vocabulary and some explanation of key ideas. The chapters touch on the meaning of many of these: revelation, symbol, silence, scripture, fears, unworthiness, worship, affirmation, God language, God concept, dreams, panic, anger, intercession, healing, culture, gender, humanity, sin, confession, absolution, forgiveness, repentance, thanksgiving, spiritual depression, withdrawal of God, the dark night of the soul, spiritual direction, sacraments, reflection, the will of God, and the goal of heaven. In these chapters I aim to explain what is meant by these terms and what place they have in our spiritual development.

## Our Relationship with God

Soul time is the opportunity to look at the time and space that we make for the development of our personal, intimate relationship with God. In accordance with Christian doctrine, God takes the initiative in engaging with us in such a relationship. Christ is essential to this relationship as the human face of God, and, like the disciples of the first century, we are called to be both followers and friends of Christ. Such a relationship is not simply for our instruction but for the development of an intimate relationship with God, born out of love, mutuality, respect, care, emotion, affection, affirmation, and sharing of ideas and empowerment.

Such a relationship with God results in an increased understanding of our own selves and our relationship to others. If either of these impedes the growth of our relationship with God—and that is likely from time to time—then we can take time out to work on this with other helpers. This makes clear the difference between spiritual direction and counseling. In the final chapter, I will discuss the roles of these helpers. A counselor may be any professional dedicated to the growth of our personality who helps us clear away any blockages that prevent attainment of maturity. A spiritual director is a skilled person dedicated to helping us develop our relationship with God until we gain the fullness of the stature of Christ in the maturity of his humanity. As we find it necessary from time to time, we can call on both counselor and director to assist us. The deeper we enter into a relationship with God, the deeper we come to see ourselves in a balanced way—as we really are and as we really can be.

So it is time to take our first step and start the journey of development. Each time we take a step it is appropriate to offer a prayer. Readers may like to use their own words or the prayers that I have collected or written. Prepare for this time of prayer with a short time of silence and an opportunity to focus on the reality of God's presence.

> *Gracious God, you have promised to give us your Holy Spirit*
> *to inspire our relationship with you.*
> *Breathe fresh energy into our spiritual life*
> *so that we may be aware of your presence,*
> *hear your encouragement and direction for us,*
> *and grow toward the person that you would have us be;*
> *for the sake of our Lord Jesus the Christ. Amen.*

# 1
# Awareness of the Presence of God

In our personal development of the soul, we must start with an awareness of the presence of God. From that beginning, we can enter more fully into a relationship with God. When I have been in conversation with those eager to make progress in their spiritual life, I have encouraged them with some appropriate questions or pointers to identify their experiences of the Divine. I have found that it does not take long before they are able to tell me about many of them. I would like to begin this chapter by sharing some of the responses I have heard over the years. You will be able to test your own experiences by comparing them with what follows. Try to think of those times when you said to yourself: "It was wonderful. God was in that experience."

## Experiencing God

### In Creation

A lot of people have described to me an experience they had of the wonder of creation. They tell me of some beautiful scene of a lake or a sunset or a tree or a mountain, and how they stood in breathless wonder of it all. The lasting impression was not the marvel of it, but the way they were aware of a divine presence. They knew the reality of God in that piece of creation. More especially, they had a sense of personal relationship to God. The words tumble out as they tell me: "I will never forget looking up at the stars on that still, clear night and feeling that the great God who created all of that was very near me. I could relate with closeness even though the heavens were so vast." They knew that God was there and that God was real. They could not give me any scientific explanation, but that did not matter. "It touched my soul," they would say. There was often a little self-consciousness in the voice, as if they were apologetic at saying something that sounded rather sentimental. Yet they were very convinced of the experience and the reality of it. There was for them a Creator God, and that God was not concerned only with the created order in general, but with that person. There was communication, there was wonder, and the experience brought joy.

## In Conversation

Then there are those who tell me of a time when they have been in conversation with another person about deep things—about the meaning of life or the best course of action to take for the future. In those conversations the persons giving me the accounts said that they felt as if God had spoken a word directly to them. They were sure that the words did not come from them. The words came from "beyond," and when they spoke, it was as if they were being addressed by the words. They were convinced that the words did not originate in their own minds. "I am sure that that was a word from God," they would tell me in a tone of confidence. They would often pause at that point and look intently at me with a question in their eyes: "Do you think God can speak to me like that?" I let the pause continue for a moment or two since I believe it is important that they find the answer to their own question before I add my confirmation that I have had similar experiences and so have many others. The Bible and the saints assure us all of its truth.

## In Holy Places

The experiences that others share with me are associated with "holy places." People tell me how they have entered a church that was empty at that moment. They felt drawn to kneel down and still their souls in silence. When they looked up, their eyes fixed on some symbol that was the mysterious presence of God for them. It was as if God was looking directly at them, eager to enter into a dialogue. The persons tell me that, in the encouragement of that presence, they felt they were able to share all that was in their heart with God. They were comforted by the support of all the prayers offered in that space over many generations. "That was a holy church," they tell me. The walls seemed to breathe with the prayers of the saints. "I knew God was beside me, and then I was sure there was the host of heaven all around me." My own experience of kneeling in the church of Santa Chiara in Assisi before the cross from the church that Saint Francis rebuilt echoed these experiences. With a multitude of pilgrims and tourists near me, I created a space around my kneeling figure and there was Christ before me—strengthening, blessing, calling me on in my spiritual journey. Yes, I am well aware that it was an old wooden cross and the figure of Christ was stylized in an Italian art form, but that is not what I "saw." This was an experience of the soul, not of the outward senses. Many have shared similar experiences with me over many years of ministry, and most people have had one or two in their lifetime. What I find is that Christians are very hesitant in speaking about them in case they are thought to be a little mad! The truth is that our souls would be starved of sustenance without some of these experiences. How can we speak of a living, generous God if that God does not give us experiences that bring excitement to our faith and joy to our souls? The answer is that we cannot, but we are not called upon to do so. God does give each one of us individually those experiences that help us best relate to God.

**In the Scriptures**

Then again, other people will tell me of a different type of experience of the presence of God. They find God as they read the pages of the scriptures—the First[1] and the New Testaments. As they ponder over the words in prayer, they have an understanding that God is explaining the meaning of the passage in relation to the immediate life of the reader. It is as if they are on the road to Emmaus and Jesus is telling them the meaning of the passage (Lk. 24:27). The words speak of the nature of God, the purpose of God, and the depth of the love of God, within the context of their life at this point. The words are a springboard for a dialogue with God that leads to action and affirmation. Some people say that they have this experience more with the words in the New Testament, but others say that the First Testament is equally a channel of the divine word for them. They have prayed that the Holy Spirit will breathe fresh wisdom and liveliness into the words, and they find that the prayer is answered as they read with patience and ponder in expectation. Sometimes these people tell me that the experience of God comes when another person is interpreting the scriptures to them—though they are always

---

[1] The First Testament is often called the Old Testament or the Hebrew Scriptures.

certain that the message came from God and not the interpreter. In some cases they have checked it out, and the interpreter has not even intended that to be the message at all.

**In Dreams**

The final example of experiences of the presence of God that I want to give at this point is one that people have been prepared to share in more recent times. They tell me of the experiences of dreams. In these dreams they have had a vision of God, or of God in Christ, with such vividness that they speak of touching as well as seeing. The tendency some years ago was to dismiss dreams as belonging to the past or due to overeating! Now dreams are regarded as part of communication—with ourselves and with spiritual powers. It is difficult to "define" dreams, but they certainly should not be dismissed. In our waking and in our sleeping we can still be open to the experiences of God. I usually find that the dream has been very vivid for those who tell me of it, and that they are convinced, after they have reflected on the dream, that it was God who had given them this experience. The dream might have contained a "vision" of God. Some even see a face or hands or a bright light or color. Others hear a voice that speaks and often repeats a number of times a clear message. There is nothing vague or unsure about such experiences in dreams. Reflecting on it in our waking moments, we are convinced that the communication was real. It makes sense to the mind as well as the heart. "God was in that dream," they will tell me as a matter of fact, not as a question or opinion. My response is to accept it and to give thanks with the person. Such an experience comes from the beyond, but not from the impossible.

## Common Principles in These Experiences

It has been good to share with you some of these experiences. Some of them find echoes in my experience, and, as I wrote them down, new joy arose in my heart. I hope that it might have been equally exciting for you as you read about the experiences of others. Everyone is different, as I have said, and there should be no jealousy because the way I experience God is not the same as you do. Yet there are similarities, and there are some basic principles behind the individual experiences. Here are some of them:

Nearly everyone in these experiences of the presence of God tells of the God *who takes the initiative* toward us. It is not that we have worked it out and discovered God for ourselves. The experience is that God came to us before we came to God. It is that we knew that God loved us first before we responded with our love for God. Often the experience came as a total surprise in the form of a blinding light, an overwhelming sense of holiness, or a feeling of being enfolded by love. Such experiences came unexpectedly from beyond or beneath us. In my deepest need, there was God. In my times of ecstatic joy, there was God. In the space of the silence I kept, there was God. The words of scripture leaped out from the page, and there was God. The discovery was one of recognition that God had found me, rather than I had unveiled God.

Another common factor in these experiences is that they all have elements of *mystery, awesomeness,* and *majesty* that sometimes feel as though they will overpower us. No one feels that the experiences could be classed as "ordinary." The sense of the holy is dominant and, even if we are not shaken with fear because the experience of God is so powerful, we still have an awareness that humility and gratitude are the only right responses to what has taken place. When we are conscious of having hurt others, or our life is in a mess, then, of course, such experiences will heighten our desire to make a fresh start. In those circumstances we may tremble until we find the gift of forgiveness bestowed upon us. Then the joy of the release from the past will be overwhelming. What is definitely common to the experience is that it is a source of wonder and delight, and yet at the same time it is beyond the powers of ordinary definition.

Most people who are Christians find that the experience is *personal.* We are not in the presence of a "force" or an abstract power. The experience is that we are in the presence of a personal Being, and Jesus Christ is the way in which this personhood is made real for us. Jesus becomes the true image of the Divine to which we as humans can more easily relate. The passages of the New Testament help us to define this picture, and through them we come to know Jesus. Our minds can picture him walking, healing, teaching, empathizing, forgiving, dying, rising, and ascending. These passages recreate for us the real person, and we can feel him there beside us. Like Saint Peter and Saint Thomas, we can "know it is the Lord."

Also common to the variety of experiences of the presence of God is the fact that the experiences can only be described as *spiritual* ones. They are conveyed to us by a deep awareness of a warm, charged, spiritual power that enfolds us. Our spirit and this Spirit become united in an embrace that we find is freedom and peace, comfort and calling, all in one. Most people struggle to put this experience into words.

It is "too deep for words," they will say; or "I know that it was real, but I can't describe it easily to you."

There is something very special about all these kinds of experiences of the presence of God, and all of them are *unique* to a particular occasion. We may have similar ones again, but each experience is unique. This can be a trap for some people as they constantly look backward to some special revelation of God to them. This pulls them backward while life is forcing them forward. For them God is always more real in the past than in the present or in the future. It is true that we cannot recapture such experiences, but they can become building blocks for our present and future relationship with God.

## Building Blocks for Relationship

Take the parallel of our ongoing appreciation of beauty. At some time in the past, we may have had this wonderful experience of a sunset, when the sun sank with a golden glow beneath the line of the ocean. All the colors and all the silhouettes of shapes were there to create the blend of beauty. Future examples of beauty were never the same as in that sunset. Our understanding of beauty was enhanced by that sunset, and our journey to find more of beauty was given a kick start. We build on that experience, recalling it from time to time to help us continue in our search. In the future we will always recognize beauty in all its variety of forms.

Likewise, we can use our previous vivid experiences of the presence of God as building blocks for our spiritual growth. By their very nature, as gifts from the God of revelation and assurance, such experiences cannot be repeated. Yet they can be remembered and affirmed with thanksgiving. Their importance and strength lie in encouraging us to enter into the presence of God in the current moment, knowing more about the God who has given us these experiences in the past. Recalling them, we can be sure that God will be there for us now.

### What Is Real for Me?

Enough about the principles behind other people's experiences of God. Now it is time to allow you to recall your own. Take a pause in the reading and think of all the times when you have said: "God was real for me at that moment." You might like to put a pad and pen beside you before you begin so that you can jot down your memories as they flood back into your mind. Feel your experience again as your memory refreshes it.

*Take Time for Yourself Here.*

Most people find it helpful to sum up this activity with a prayer of thanksgiving. You might like to look at your whole list quickly if you have written it down on a pad. The following prayer will probably sound similar to any you have made up for yourself.

> *Wonderful God, I thank you for all the experiences that you have given me of yourself. You have allowed me to enter into such a relationship of mystery and understanding with you that I can only marvel that you, Holy God, would take notice of me and, even more, tell me that you love and care about me. In light and power I have come to know you. In gentleness and grace you have found me. In the face of Jesus I have seen your nature. Your Spirit calls to my spirit, and I find in you all that I long for. Help me to build on these experiences and move on to deepen this relationship. Then I can call you "My God"; and you can affirm that I am your beloved child, companion, and friend—for that is what I want to be, now and forever. Amen.*

## Practical Steps for the Relationship

Now that we have some basic building blocks for our relationship with God, let us see how we can take some practical steps to deepen this relationship.

This book is called *Soul Time* because time and the soul are the two basic ingredients for the development of our relationship with God. The soul recognizes that there is a spiritual side to our nature as human beings. To mention time is to point to the fact that we must be prepared to allocate time for this relationship to grow. In addition to time, we will need to create space and will probably find that there are certain aids that assist us to enter into the presence of God.

### Time

First, let me make some comments about time. The time span does not have to be long, but it does have to be intentional. It will be focused time, when you concentrate on the purpose for using this time to deepen and develop your relationship with God. It will also help if the allotment of time can be regular. This could be daily, or weekly, or a longer period of time once a month. The art is to set realistic goals and to try out a system to see what makes for progress. The amount of progress is the test rather than just occupying the time spaces that you have allocated. What is true is that most people find this soul time so enriching and enjoyable, that it gives such strength, that they would feel the gap deeply if deprived of the chance to make this time available.

## Space

The space you will need for soul time is best if it is created around you rather than provided for you. As long as you can shut out what is unhelpful to your relationship with God, you are free to enter into this space as soon as you create it purposefully. Some people desire a "regular holy space" and go apart to enter it. Others like to create the space in the middle of their normal setting of life. They take the opportunity while traveling on a bus or train to work or while walking, exercising the soul as well as the body. In this space, we recognize that God is there with us, and we are able to relate with ease with our God.

## Aids to Worship

Having allocated time and space for the task, we prepare ourselves to enter our relationship with God. Many people like to have aids to assist them in doing this. They will use a candle, a picture, an icon, or a statue of a saint. None of these are ends in themselves but act like entry doors into the presence of God. They draw us in so that we can focus on the reality of the presence of God—and the qualities of that presence: peace, light, companionship, hope, joy, fulfillment, unity, forgiveness, and openness to dialogue. Others find that the words of scripture are the aid they need to bring them into the presence of God. They may have their favorite verses marked in their Bible or commit them to memory. For them these verses recapture the presence of God and bring new strength and joy. Another symbol that many Christian people use is the cross. It may stand on a table or hang on the wall. Its gift or purchase will always have special meaning to add to that which is always there: the recollection of the undying love of God, the symbol of our calling by God at our baptism, and, with an "open" cross, the sign of resurrection and its victory over sin and death. We might also have a cross that we can hold in our hands or place before our eyes in times of trial and pain. I treasure such a cross made of olive wood from the old trees in the garden of Gethsemane. It was given to me by friends in Jerusalem at the time of my consecration as bishop. Bishops certainly need something to hang on to in their times of testing and decision making!

I find it most helpful to have a variety of aids about me in the space I create for my times of relationship to God. Most of these objects are associated with events and places in which I have felt very close to God's presence. There is an olive wood cross from Jerusalem, a picture of Saint Francis from Assisi, a candle from the cathedral shop in Vienna, and a Bible given to me at my confirmation. The only warning is that these objects are not there to draw me back in nostalgia to the past event, but to draw me into the presence of God here and now by affirming that God will reveal the Being of God to me again.

**Keeping Things Fresh**

This is a good point at which to make another observation. We will soon become bored with the relationship if we get into a rut. Merely repeating something will not lead to development. You will find that the delight in the relationship will soon dry up. This is true of human relationships and is equally true of our relationship with God. So go on trying out different ways of relating to God and experiencing the presence of God. If up to now your relationship has been focused mostly on the experience of the God of creation, then add to that by using the scriptures to picture Jesus in a variety of settings— and then relate to him as your friend and guide. Ask him questions; seek to understand why he is acting as he is; find out more about Jesus from his friends and disciples; ask Peter or Mary of Magdala why they found Jesus so attractive and how he challenged them; ask John or Andrew in what ways Jesus led them into a life of larger fulfillment. If you do this, you will find that you soon start sharing all of your life with Jesus, all your hopes and fears and all your deepest longings.

**Spirit to Spirit**

If the previous paragraph is how you usually experience the presence of God, then it is probably time to discover the experience of God as Spirit. This is when deep calls to deep, between God's Spirit and your spirit. Experience God as the source of spiritual qualities such as love, joy, peace, kindness, self-control, hope, fulfillment, purpose, beauty, light, and power. You may find here that music is a wonderful aid to such an experience. Music speaks to the soul and aids this Spirit-to-spirit relationship. Other people find that the depth of silence allows the spirit space to dwell within the Divine Spirit. The experience of the Spirit has energy and vigor, and then peace and silence as its two polarities. It is good to balance the one with the other from time to time.

Christians come to understand that all these various experiences of God are complementary and, held together, help us understand the height, depth, and breadth of the love of God for us. When we experience the Spirit, it is the Spirit of Christ that we meet. This Spirit of God is not detached from the personal, but is another form of the relationship with the one God. Equally, the relationship with Christ brings us into the relationship with God, the Holy One, the majestic Creator, and the caring parent. If we want to relate to the whole of God, then we will be always ready to move on in the discovery of what is yet to be revealed to us. This is the exciting side of our willingness to enter into this relationship with God: There is always more to come—more depth, more height, more width—to the love of God that is the means and essence of the relationship. Pause now and recommit yourself to this "moving on" process with a prayer that is based on these lines:

*God of the pilgrim, you delight in discovery. We thank you for the joy of all that is new. Help us never to think that the past has more of your presence than the future—however young or old we are. Keep our eyes open to further experiences of yourself in all your complex richness. Hold our hand as we journey on with you, and give us signs of your continuing presence and power. Make us secure enough in your love to be free to move beyond the restrictive boundaries of what is familiar, so that we may know you more fully, day by day. Amen.*

Remember that the object of our relationship with God is an openness to God's revelation of Godself to us and to a growing unity of our wills, so that we *willingly* do what is in tune with the divine purpose for our lives and the life of all humanity. This is the growth that we long for in our personal lives, and when we finally know we are on that pathway, we feel that we are "in heaven." We will do everything we can to stay on this pathway. If we slip from this "way," then we will want to tell God how sorry we are that we have spoiled the relationship by our arrogance or apathy. We will confess our denial of God or our hurt to another human being. We will seek forgiveness for our self-centered pride and our disrespect in taking everything for granted.

## Moses' Experience of God

At this point I want to explore the experience of the presence of God as told to us in scripture. Moses' experience, as it is related to us in Exodus 3:1–15, was pivotal for the Hebrew people as they developed their relationship with God and made new discoveries. It is also an experience that in many ways mirrors the elements that are common in our own experiences of God. I am sure that is why it is recorded in the way it is. Here, then, are some of the steps in the experience, which may be similar to your own pathway into a relationship with God:

- The experience of God comes to us in the midst of our everyday life. Exodus records that Moses was carrying out his task of caring for his father-in-law's flocks when he encountered God. The writer also makes the point that the experience of God can come in a place where others have previously been conscious of the presence of God. Moses was grazing his flocks at Horeb, the mountain of God, which was known to be a sacred spot.

- The story tells that the experience of God came at the initiative of God. Moses did not set out to find God. It was God who met Moses in the course of life's journey. This first experience that Moses had of God came in the form of an event in the created order, through the observance of nature. There was a bush burning with fire, but remarkably the bush itself was not on fire. Moses stood in wonder at this strange occurrence in nature.

- As is common for most of us in these circumstances, Moses had to "turn aside and look." Moses could have passed by, attributing the fire to some natural cause and event. He could have told himself that there was nothing important to investigate in this situation. The writer makes clear that Moses had to give himself the opportunity to go aside and reflect if he was to gain a spiritual insight from this natural experience. This applies to us as well.

- Once Moses was in a receptive mood, God could start a relationship on a person-to-person basis. Moses found that God was not in the fire, but in the still, small voice. The fire was merely the event that caused Moses to be ready to listen. When God called, Moses responded with a willingness to enter into the relationship.

- Very quickly Moses was aware of the awesomeness of God. Here was a relationship with a God who was holy and eternal. The story gives us a sign that Moses felt like that. He had to remove his sandals to show that he realized he was standing on holy ground. It was not that the ground was holy in itself, but that the ground was holy because it was the place of encounter with the holiness of God. For us in our generation we might say that we knelt down, or stood still in silence, as we felt the holiness of some sacred place that held the memories of the presence of God for others before us.

- Who was this holy God? All the steps so far had prepared Moses for this revelation of who God was. God revealed to Moses that there was a continuity in the experience of God between the past and the present. The God that confronted Moses was the same God who had been known by the generations before Moses—to his father and his ancestors—to Abraham, Isaac, and Jacob. The individualism of the experience cannot be detached from the experiences of others, past and present. God may address us personally but always remains the God of our community and our humanity as a whole.

- Such an awareness of the holiness of God at first overwhelmed Moses. The writer says that Moses hid his face and was too frightened to look at God. This is common for many of us, and it is only the encouragement of Jesus that gives us the confidence to look into the face of God. In Christ we are made children of God able, with simple trust to look into the face of our Abba God.

- After discovering who God is, Moses is shown how God acts. He is assured that God sees, that God hears, that God feels, that God acts to save and bring the lives of God's people to their joyful fulfillment. God has seen the pain, God has heard the cries, God feels for the suffering, and God has *acted*. That is the point of the tense of the verb in verse 8.

- Yet this God does not act alone. God calls humanity into partnership to fulfill the salvation history. Our experience of God will lead us, too, into activity with and for God. Our experiences of the presence of God are never an end in themselves. They lead to the fulfillment of God's purpose in our lives and in the lives of our communities. As the experience of God initially fills us with awe, the call of God will initially fill us with fear and apprehension about how we could possibly do the things we are asked to do. So Moses asks: "How can I do these things?"

- It is at this point that we find the experience of God strengthens and affirms us as we take up the challenge of action. We know and experience God *with* us. God's spiritual energy and gifting equips us for service.
- Finally, God promises Moses more experiences in the future. The promise God gives to Moses is that this place will always be holy. God will be there to be worshiped "on this mountain." In his relationship with God, Moses will understand that this is a relationship of "worth"—the worship of God. Moses and the people will offer thanks and praise to the God who has acted for them, and God will acknowledge Moses as an important person with a role to play in the unfolding history of humanity.

You can feel the joy in Moses' heart and the excitement of the experience. Then comes the *but.* You can almost hear Moses saying: "Wait a minute, God. Don't go away, I have just one question—What can I call you, what's your name?" It is surprising in this part of the account that the writer shows us that God is willing to let Moses know the very heart and personality of God. There is a sharp contrast here between verse 6 where Moses covers his face in fear and the question Moses dares to ask in verse 13, "God, what is your name?"

In the answer God shares with Moses the essence of the divine nature. "I AM—who I am; what I am; and what I will be." God's revelation is both an answer to the question and a mystery that leads to other questions. By expressing the name as the verb "to be" God both satisfies us with the starting point and draws us further into the mystery. As humanity we can never contain God by knowing all about God. It is God who knows all about us. But as human beings God has chosen to relate to us, and therefore we are privileged to have some understanding of who God is. God is "alive, active, creative." God is the source of life, power, and energy. God is the personal "I am," the one who is eternal—who was and is and is to come. And as we discover in Jesus, God is "Immanuel"—God with us. Our experience of God as Holy Spirit also tells us that God is there and that God is there for us. All these understandings flow from the exploration of the root wrapped up in the verb "to be." Power, presence, and personality are at the heart of all our experiences of God. This is what Moses discovered in his encounter with God on the holy mountain, and this was the experience that drew him on to all the relationships with God that are portrayed in the rest of Exodus.

God's invitation to us is to make the same discovery for ourselves:

to move from observation to acknowledgment;
to relationship, partnership, affirmation, revelation,
and to worship.

Keep a space of silence about you now and be ready to hear the voice of God speaking to you in love, affirmation, calling, and empowerment. Then you might like to end with this prayer:

*God, you come to meet us in our everyday experiences*
*and to transform them into moments of holiness and truth.*
*We thank you for your willingness to enter into relationship with us*
*as we are,*
*and to recreate in us what we can be.*
*Help us, gracious God, to cherish this relationship,*
*and to be open to receive your revelation and companionship.*
*God of many names but of one being, we worship you with mind*
*as well as heart,*
*with understanding as well as emotion.*
*Help us to reflect on your nature, so that we can enter more deeply*
*into your heart,*
*and there find harmony of purpose with your divine will.*
*Ready us for the tasks to which you call us,*
*and empower us with your divine energy and strength.*
*Above all else, help us to put time and space aside*
*to enjoy your company*
*and to know and love you more and more;*
*for you are the God of our ancestors, and you are now our God*
*forever and ever. Amen.*

# 2

# Relating to the God of the Scriptures

The Holy Scriptures have always been a source of inspiration for those seeking to deepen their spiritual relationship with their God. Various passages give illustrations of how key figures developed their relationship with God, and other passages help us to clarify the nature of the God who is revealed in these encounters. For Christians Jesus defines the nature of God, and so reading the New Testament is both our duty and delight as we seek to relate to God.

The scriptures are, on the one hand, "historical," in the sense that they were written in previous generations. They tell of God's actions in the past and of the people involved in those actions. The scriptures, on the other hand, have always been "living" documents, because they not only shed light on the past but also on the present circumstances. Since the nature of God is constant, the examples of relationship and revelation in the past help us to interpret the mind and heart of God in the present situation. We see this principle already at work in the way some passages of scripture were revised even before they were recorded in the form that has been passed down to us. For example, editors drew parallels between the exodus and the return from exile in the First Testament, and there was a reapplication of the truths contained in the parables of Jesus in the New Testament. For the compilers of Holy Scripture, God's word was constantly alive and could be applied to the context of every generation and culture.

With this in mind, we can look at a small selection of passages in the scriptures to see how they can help us in our spiritual journey.

Our experiences of God may not be "dressed in the same clothes" as these experiences in scripture, but in them we will recognize the same God as is revealed to us and see that they contain many similarities to our reactions within our relationship with God.

## Age and Youth Experience God

The first passage I have chosen is from the First Testament—1 Samuel 3. It tells how youth and age complement one another in the experience of God, and how relationship is followed by a sense of responsibility.

Samuel is still a young boy when he first encounters God in a direct relationship. He had been brought up to *know about* God. Now this account tells how he had a personal relationship *with* God. This is a vital step in the pilgrimage of any person, young or old, but it is especially important for younger people to make this transition from knowing about religion to knowing God in a personal way for themselves. On the other hand, Eli was an old man who had a continuing relationship with God through the ups and downs of his long life. Eli's eyesight was failing, but of more importance was the fact that his spiritual discernment was failing. He was unable to discipline the sons in his own household, who should have taken over his religious responsibilities of making the connection between the people and their God. The failure meant that their priestly responsibilities would have to be taken away from them. God would raise up a new line of priests and prophets to help all the people truly relate to God. Despite this failure, Eli still had a part to play in helping the young boy Samuel to recognize the experience of God that would come to him in the night.

Samuel's experience came as an inner voice, and at first he found it difficult to believe that it could be anything other than a human voice. He was so sure of this that he went to Eli. "Surely it was the old man who was calling me," you can hear him thinking to himself. In the end Eli had the wisdom, born out of experience, to help the young boy to recognize that there is an inner voice that comes from God to which we must listen. One of the treasures of this passage is that it encourages young Christians to check out their experiences with older Christians who have traveled this road before. It is also a reminder to older Christians of their role in affirming vivid experiences of God among the young.

Once Eli has pointed out to Samuel the source of the voice, Samuel readies himself to enter into a dialogue with the Almighty. It is important to note that God is not willing to force such a dialogue on anyone until he or she is ready to listen and respond. This is a two-way relationship in which respect and patience are essential. The passage helps us to see that God keeps calling humanity into a relationship, but God will not force any of us to listen. We must want God to speak with us. A major step forward occurs when Samuel is able to say: "Speak, Lord, for your servant is listening." In those words we find the acknowledgment of the appropriate roles in the relationship. God is God, holy and supreme, whose will is to be done on earth as it is in heaven. The human role is to act in obedience to this will, which is for the good of the individual and of the whole community. In the New Testament, Jesus reveals that the relationship has a further dimension. We are not to think of ourselves only as servants but also as friends, drawn into a partnership of responsibility, because the Spirit shares with us the mind of God. Fundamental to any relationship with God is human willingness to listen and obey. Your relationship with God finds a new dimension when you too are able to say as a servant and friend of God: "Speak, Lord, for I am ready to listen."

## Person-to-Person Encounter

Samuel's experience indicates to us that the relationship with God is a person-to-person encounter. Samuel speaks to God as he would to Eli. God speaks to Samuel in words that he can understand. Later, in Jesus, we come to see the full human face of God, but even in this First Testament passage the voice of God communicates clearly to Samuel. In our inner dialogue with God, we too can hear the warmth of the words of comfort and the sharpness of the words of challenge. This dialogue is within our capabilities because God has made us for this relationship. It is natural to us as God's own creation, human but capable of dialogue with the Divine.

The outcome of this encounter with God is that Samuel has the courage to take responsibility for acting on the message he has heard. With the respect of youth for age, Samuel waits with a mixture of faith and fear for Eli's invitation to reveal the message from God. Now it is Samuel who waits for Eli's willingness to enter into the dialogue. It was hard for Samuel to deliver the message from God. It was even harder for Eli to hear it, words of truth though it may have been. But God's work must be done, and faithfulness and honesty are required from us all. Righteousness is more important than long service, and sometimes youth has to accept heavy responsibility to fulfill the purpose of God. Such is the way that God requires.

## God's Holiness and Power

The second passage I have chosen comes from Isaiah 6. Here it is not the inner voice that prompts the discovery of a relationship with God, but external circumstances. There is a crisis in the nation. The king has died. The nation is divided. The gap between rich and poor has widened into a gulf. In the chaos of a broken nation, who will take charge and restore righteousness? Isaiah goes into the house of God to pray and meditate on this state of affairs. If there is a God, why does God not take charge and put things right? Many a person has struggled in similar circumstances with the thoughts that Isaiah had. They may be our thoughts too whenever we face a crisis. We ask ourselves: "Where is God? Why does God not take charge?"

In the midst of his reflection, Isaiah had an "overwhelming" experience of God's holiness and power. There, in the place where God's people were promised the presence of God in good times and in bad, Isaiah became certain that there was a God who reigned over the created order. Yes, this God in heaven may be high above us, but the signs of God's authority ("the hem of his robe") were spread all around us right here on earth. This God had as servants heavenly creatures who acknowledged the holiness of God and served the purposes of God. This God had the power to shake up the affairs of humanity and to break down its false foundations. Isaiah's experiences were directly related to the circumstances of his day. God did not keep at a distance, but was involved in the affairs of the nation that claimed a special relationship with God. That was the clear message that came to this man as he wrestled and prayed for his nation in its turmoil. When we see our nation in turmoil, lacking direction and vision, torn apart by greed and intolerance, where everyone aims at his or her own welfare and ignores the needs of others, have we the faith of Isaiah in God's power to act and restore righteousness and justice? That challenge may be a new turning point in the growth of our relationship with God.

As we examine this passage, we find that the encounter moves from the corporate to the personal. We are reminded that the community is made up of individuals, each of whom must accept some responsibility for the common state of affairs. In the presence of God we cannot simply blame others for the wickedness. We too have to accept our part in the disaster. Isaiah models this for us all. "Woe is me" is not a cry of self-pity, but an acceptance of responsibility. I too have contributed to the trivializing of God's name. My lips are unclean because I have allowed the names of false gods to pass over them. What will happen to us all? Isaiah discovers that repentance can lead to renewal. God is in charge and has the energy and the power to make dramatic changes to the situation—both for the individual and for the nation. Isaiah experiences pardon and cleansing for himself. The lips that have betrayed God can be transformed into lips that honor and speak for God. From a renewed heart comes a willingness to serve God. Even though God is in charge and God's heavenly messengers are active, God still needs earthly messengers. Our yes is vital to God's plans of restoration and righteousness.

Again we see the relationship mature to the point where the encounter leads to the acceptance of partnership in activity between God and the disciple. Empowered by the experience of God, Isaiah can speak for God and point the nation in a new direction. The nation may be deaf to the message, but the words of Isaiah have gone on speaking to generations of those who have ears to hear. For our relationship to develop, we must not only say with Samuel: "Speak, for your servant is listening;" we must also say: "Here I am, Lord, ready to do what you will to bring a new way of justice and peace into being."

Pause now and give yourself time to speak these words to God in your own personal way. Here is a prayer which you might like to use before you continue with the next part of this chapter.

*Gracious God,*
*thank you for continuing to call me into relationship with you.*
*Open the ears of my soul to hear your words to me.*
*Open my heart to accept your cleansing and renewing love.*
*Open my hands to receive the gifts of your Spirit.*
*Open my lips to speak your words of truth that challenge and*
  *change lives.*
*Stand with me as I stand up for righteousness and care of the*
  *needy,*
  *and then empower me to play my part in your reshaped world,*
  *for I am ready to be your servant and your friend,*
  *now and always. Amen.*

## Firsthand Experience

We move on to the New Testament to examine a passage that will give us another example of an experience of God to inspire and affirm our own relationship with God. The First Testament prophets had spoken with and for God, but they never claimed to be God incarnate. The last of the prophets, John the Baptist, had the dual task of preparing the road for people to travel to encounter God in Jesus and of pointing to this person in whom we would find a living and loving relationship with the one true God.

Many people tell of how they have heard about God from the words of others. However, they are aware that this is always a secondhand experience until they are drawn into a different type of relationship with God. This is a relationship of deep empathy, understanding, and mutuality. By relating to Jesus Christ they discover a new type of "knowing," that is, a relationship with all the attributes of an in-depth, person-to-person encounter. John the Baptist is the bridge into this new knowledge. He begins by telling everyone what God wants for the world and about the fresh start we must all make. The message is delivered in stern tones from "on high." Then he points us to Jesus, and in him we find the relationship transformed from "out there" to "beside you."[1] Jesus draws us into a relationship of friendship in which respect, mutuality, and common understanding are the distinguishing marks.

## Relationship through Baptism

The passage that reflects this change is found in Matthew 3. The chapter begins with a call to get ready for a new revelation of the rule of God. This call is symbolized (or sacramentalized) by a baptism in water and the Spirit. This was to be the new sign of cleansing and empowerment to do the will of God. The chapter concludes with the baptism of Jesus. This takes place not for his personal cleansing, but because he fully identifies with the community of God, which needs renewing. We have seen such a link between corporate and personal responsibility in the passage from the prophet Isaiah. The righteousness of the people of God can only be attained when we all feel so closely linked to the whole community that their pain is our pain, and we turn with them from the ways of evil to the ways of righteousness and truth. In this gospel passage the baptismal experience reaches a climax in the affirmation of Jesus' relationship (and ours in him) with God. Jesus is revealed as "my beloved son"—words that express intimacy within a family relationship. The Spirit binds Father and Son, Parent and Child, together.

---

[1] This is one interpretation of the words, "The kingdom of God has come *near*," in v. 2.

For us the voice of God may begin with a call to repentance and renewal, but it will conclude with an affirmation that "in Christ" we are the "beloved son or daughter" of our heavenly Father. From Jesus we learn how to develop this relationship. This scripture passage tells us of our place in God's family and of God's initiative and generosity. In baptism we can hear the declaration that God has given us this place as a gift. We know that we do not deserve it and that we cannot earn it. It is given to us freely as we come to trust in Christ's redemptive love for us. Now it is our task to live up to the role that has been chosen for us and that we gladly accept. We learn to live in this family. We learn to accept our responsibilities and to enjoy our privileges. We learn to have respect for all our sisters and brothers and to work closely with them because they share the same relationship with God in Christ and are filled with the same Spirit of God.

The passage raises for us the issue of the place of the sacrament of baptism as part of our relationship with God. How important is it for us, and how important is it for the community in which we live? I hope that this passage from Matthew has helped you to see baptism in a new light. It is not only a sacrament that affirms God's love, call, and challenge to us personally, but it is also our identification with the whole Christian community. Baptism is a sign of God's activity among us. It is the call of God to humanity to enter into a full relationship with God and also a pledge by humanity to live in the power of the Spirit in the way that God intended for us all: as God's family, relating to one another with respect and mutual care. To be baptized or not is not solely an individual decision, for it has many corporate implications. Baptism is the way in which God and humanity express their mutual responsibilities and form the covenant that is both individual and corporate. Baptism links us to the family of God, the church, in such a way that the church supports the growth of the relationship and the person baptized supports the efforts of the church to be part of the implementation of the kingdom of God. If you are not baptized, then I would encourage you to speak with the leaders of your local church about this opportunity both for you and for them.

As you think about that key issue, pause and listen to God's words of affirmation: "You are my beloved child. You are the delight of my heart."

At your baptism, your brothers and sisters said (or will say) to you: "Child of God, blessed in the Spirit, welcome to the family of Christ." Take a moment to let that affirmation bring you joy and happiness.

### Insight into God

It is Saint John's gospel, with its mature thinking about the relationship between Jesus and God, that can move us one step further in our understanding of our relationship with God. If you have a Bible beside you, look up the passage in John 14:8–17.

There Philip begins with a request that is frequently on the lips of us all: "Show us the Father." At one time or another, we all want to have God shown plainly to us. Living by faith and not by sight is a struggle most of the time. We may long for a clear revelation of God that will leave no doubt in our minds about its reality. We may want God to interrupt our lives and break in with such a vision of God that we have no responsibility about interpreting the experience. We may long for certainty about God in a material way that removes any need for us to exercise faith. In his reply Jesus puts such longings into perspective: "In my words and in my actions you do have an insight into God." In the person of Jesus it is possible for us to "humanize" our understanding of the nature and will of God. If we find it hard to see God in human form, as some people did who met Jesus in the flesh, then Jesus tells us that the actions of love, justice, compassion, wholeness, and forgiveness can assure us of the presence and power of God. In Christ and through the activity of God we find that the relationship with God grows to maturity. When that begins to happen, the promise of Christ is a little startling: "Through faith in me, you will do my works and even greater works." Out of the relationship will come empowerment to carry out the works of God.

That is where the relationship involves the Spirit of God. In this way God will support us, be present with us, and share power with us. This Spirit will help us to discover the truth—about God, about ourselves, and about our tasks in the world. This Spirit so enters our inner being, our soul, that the Spirit makes a home in our heart and dwells there. The relationship enters a point of permanence and unity. God does not come and go in our lives. God dwells with us, in us, and works the works of mercy and justice through us. Indeed this is a mystery, for it stretches our understanding, but it will gradually become a truth for us.

## Encounter with Light

The symbol of *light* links mystery and truth. The source of light is always beyond definition, and yet the beam of light at its focus clearly illuminates an object so that we can see it for what it is. In Acts 9

(vv. 3–9 and 17–19 are the heart of the passage) Saint Paul encounters Christ as *light*. This light both illuminates and blinds. The light is the flash of truth in the inner mind. Until he had this encounter, Paul had confused the facts about Jesus. He had regarded him as the enemy of all that he believed was true about God. He regarded this Jesus as a liar, falsely claiming that he was the Messiah. Paul considered that Jesus had broken all the religious rules that he had been taught. But Paul had gotten it wrong about Jesus, and he had to be stunned by the light of the truth. Paul discovered in this startling experience that this Jesus, whose followers he had been persecuting, was really the true representative of God, and as Lord he was the one who was right and had to be obeyed. Paul had to come to grips with a new reality about the truth. A full U-turn was required.

We too will find that as we think deeply about the ideas that Jesus sets forth in the gospel record, some of our ideas about God will have to change. All of us have a U-turn to make. The light of the gospel will shatter some of our preconceptions. As we read more of scripture, we must be open to its challenges to our thinking and behavior.

The account makes clear that at first Paul was so stunned that he could not see and he could not eat. His physical body reflected his spiritual condition. It is often true that our encounter with God can be a fearful experience that leaves us shaken. Yet searing light and challenge are followed by healing and strength. That is the encouragement we can find in this passage. God does not shock us unless it is necessary. We may think how terrible it was for Paul at the time, but in the long-term it was both necessary and totally beneficial, not only for Paul, but for God's purposes in the world.

The agent of God's healing and strength was a human being who also found he had to do a U-turn concerning who should be thought of as an enemy of God. As so many Christians are currently affected by persecution in our world, this story resonates with their experiences. They too feel called to minister to those who oppose them. Poor Ananias is called to come face-to-face with the "enemy" and to minister to him. Bewildered but obedient, he goes and is the instrument of God's healing and empowerment for Paul. Through the Holy Spirit Paul's blindness, both physical and spiritual, is healed, and a new journey of relationship with Jesus begins. As we saw in the passage from Matthew, such an experience is outwardly sealed by baptism. Paul learns of his status as a child of God, and the Spirit dwells in him to empower him for his later work as the apostle to the Gentile peoples. His inability to eat is also overcome, and he shares food with his new family. Some commentators see in this a reference to the holy communion, the sacramental food for the Christian family. In the strength of this food Paul can begin his period of deepening his newfound relationship with Jesus Christ and with the rest of the community of disciples. For Paul an experience of Christ was always bound up with the experience of his fellow Christians. Christ and his church were one, head and body linked in one fellowship of the Spirit. To live was to live in Christ, and to live in Christ was to be a member of the body of Christ, the church.

Paul's experience on the road to Damascus was like a flash of lightning across a darkened sky. Many others have had similar experiences over the years. Yet by no means have all had this type of experience. For others the experience of God has come like the light of the dawning day—slowly unfolding in a continuum of tiny experiences until it is possible to say, "I see, but there was no particular moment when I gained such sight." It must also be remembered that Paul tells us himself that such an "awakening" was followed by a long period of reflection (Gal. 1:17–18). A turning point in one's life is followed by a period of learning and consolidation. It is very important to see such experiences in perspective. For a relationship with God always takes time to mature. It may begin suddenly and then require a period of consolidation, or it may grow gradually, working its way in stages toward maturity. Many of us believe that the relationship will only find ultimate fulfillment when we have experienced the reality of resurrection. Then the soul will be fully free to enter into a union of delight and dedication within the heart and will of God.

## Seeing Things Anew

The final passage comes from the last book in the New Testament, Revelation. This collection of visions, warnings, advice, and dreams seems to have been gathered in a time of persecution. Life on earth was so full of misery and terror that a faithful believer was sure that a gracious God would have a plan to start everything again, ridding the world of wickedness and restoring the reign of God. There will be times on our pilgrimage when we too want a new start, new words of hope and encouragement, and an assurance that God will overcome darkness and death. In a later chapter of this book, I will explore these issues more fully. Here it is enough to note that scripture provides us with examples of every type of experience in our relationship with God.

Earlier in the chapter, I spoke of the experience of "hearing" God. In Revelation 21:1–8, the experience is of "seeing" God. The writer saw many "new" things. He saw a new heaven and a new earth. He saw a new Jerusalem. He saw the old ways of death, crying, and pain pass away, making way for the new creation of God. There the tears will be wiped away, the thirsty will have water, and the orphaned will know that God is their parent. Out of the relationship with God a new hope is born, not because we are taken away from the world, but because the world itself will be transformed by the presence of God in its midst. "The home of God is among mortals," and God "himself will be with them" (Rev. 21:3). In our longing for a better world we often pray to God to take us out of the situation. God's response is to assure us that God is *in* the situation beside us. Our relationship with God transforms the situation, but does not remove it. We find that in the pain there is a new peace and, after the tears, a clearer sight. Death has lost its sting in resurrection, but death belongs to mortality, and we cannot avoid it. God walks with us through the valley of the shadow of death, for we cannot go around it. Out of our relationship grows the strength, with God, to face the whole of life as it is and as it shall be. This is the true hope that is found by the followers of the crucified Lord. Good Friday and Easter are both experiences in which God is fully present and fully revealed as love.

## Summary

What have we learned from this short review of six passages in scripture, both from the First Testament and the New Testament? Most important of all, we have learned that God has made us capable of entering into a relationship of love, knowledge, and mutual will with God. An experience of God is the norm. It is not the exception, just for particularly holy or worthy people. This should encourage us all to develop our own relationship to God in a way which is most suitable for us. We also note that the experiences come in a variety of forms. Some grow out of "voices" and some from "visions"; some come from consideration of the circumstances; and some develop as naturally as they do in any human family or friendship. However, all of them move to a personal relationship where there is mutual respect and an understanding of appropriate roles. Every experience of God leads on to the acceptance of responsibility to play a full part in the maintenance of righteousness and works of care and compassion. Such works are empowered by the Holy Spirit and become affirmations of the presence of God in our lives. The scripture passages have also taught us that God seeks to abide with us, and the relationship is a permanent one. We do not need to fear that we will wake up one morning and find God absent from our lives. We have also learned that as we live in God, so we take our place in God's family, not only for the help it gives us, but also for the strength we can add to the corporate whole. The scriptures have shown us that we must constantly check out our understanding of God and of God's will against the words and actions of Jesus. In Christ we find the pattern of our relationship and the pattern for our lives. Christ is the human face and voice of God, who has promised that with his Spirit we will be able to carry on his works of mercy and forgiveness, bringing new life and hope to others. That pattern will help us to face our pain and death and lead us on in hope to our resurrection and eternal life.

## Warning!

What a lot we have learned from a few short passages! What delight we can have in letting the scriptures continue to enhance our relationship with God. However, at this point I must add one or two warnings about reading the Bible. Our relationship with God can be distorted by two factors in particular.

The first factor is any attempt to select small passages of scripture and take them out of context with the whole of the material. It is possible to get a very distorted view of God by the random selection of verses from any part of the Bible. It is as if we took a glorious painting, examined in detail some of the parts, and then told ourselves that we understood the whole picture from these small pieces. Some verses of the Bible taken in isolation will give you a picture of a God of war who is out to tramp in the blood of his enemies; of a God who can make things happen like magic; of a distant God who doesn't want to know about the troubles of human beings; of a God who has a list of regulations about what we eat and do, and then rewards and punishes us for such trivialities; of a God who is going to bring the world to an end any moment because of the wickedness of humanity; or of a God who has a preference for some people over others. When faced with these small "frames" of the total picture we need a good guide who has had the time and skill to study the whole and see where the pieces fit in. There are many good written commentaries and many good pastors in local congregations who are there to help us understand God in a truer or fuller sense. As in the case of Samuel and Eli, let those with long experience help those who are beginning on the journey.

The second cause of distortion comes from the projection of some failed human experiences into our relationship with God. For some it will never be easy to speak of God as "Father," or maybe even "Parent," because the human relationship with these figures has been so severely damaged. We may even find ourselves frightened of God because we have been threatened with God's judgment by some human authority figure. We may have been so rejected by human beings that we do not even know the proper meaning of the words *love* or *forgiveness*. We may be filled with deep anger at God because we were told that God had "taken away" someone whom we loved profoundly. Many human experiences can become barriers to the development of our relationship to God; so too can false teachings about religion. We may have had terrible experiences of learning in a school or church setting. Jesus may have been portrayed to us as a weak goody-goody who was totally out of touch with life or whose teaching made no sense at all for our modern world. The name "Jesus" may be associated with swearing and violence in the home or on the street. All of this needs to be cleared away before we can make good progress on our spiritual journey. Be assured that there are those in your local Christian community who can help you and that the scriptures themselves make clear that God is always ready to give us the gift of a new beginning and strength to face what is required to release the past. My encouragement to you is not to be frightened about telling a person you can trust about these obstacles and, together in the power of the Holy Spirit, to put them behind you. In the next chapter you will find some advice about dealing with experiences that raise fears in us.

Having set forth those two warnings, we can put them to one side and reaffirm in prayer the encouragement that the scriptures have given us for the growth of our relationship with God.

## A Prayer for the Gift of Interpretation

*God of wisdom,*
*you have revealed yourself to your people in every generation.*
*We praise you for those who have shared their experiences with us*
*through the pages of scripture.*
*Help us, by the Spirit of interpretation,*
   *to learn from these experiences*
*so that we too might know you and love you.*
*Give us the strength to understand your will and to do your work,*

*that in all things we may follow the pattern of Jesus Christ
and so glorify your name, now and always.
Amen.*

# 3
# Dealing with Our Fears

At the end of the previous chapter, I mentioned that there would be things that distorted our understanding of God and prevented us from deepening our relationship with God. It is time now to look more closely at what might block progress in our spiritual development and stop us from developing our relationship with God. I have therefore called this chapter "Dealing with Our Fears."

## Fear of God

For many people, fear is the very human response that they have when they think of God's presence. They focus on the almighty power of God, and, in the presence of mystery, strange events, and the sense of God's majesty, they feel overcome with awe. We have seen this recorded in some of the passages of Holy Scripture that we have examined. There is a proper sense in which it is right that human beings like us stand in awe of God. It breaks down our arrogance that we are in charge of our world. It makes us face up to our frailty and mortality. It tells us that our knowledge of things is always going to be limited. It makes us abruptly aware of a standard of behavior that is higher than the lowest common denominator of ethical human conduct. It is a good starting place for us to acknowledge that there is a Being who is responsible for the created order, who is guiding its development toward the purpose for which it was created. We are well aware that fear between human beings is not a good basis for a relationship that should be born out of respect and mutuality. A relationship based on fear leaves one party dependent on the other, and the imposed nature of the relationship does not allow freedom in which love can operate. Neither is fear a good basis for an ongoing relationship with our Creator and God.

The scriptures declare love to be at the very heart of the nature of God. It is out of love that God approaches us to enter into the relationship. It was out of love that God took the initiative in sending the Son to share our humanity and redeem it. Mature love is said to cast out fear because there is nothing that love cannot face. Fear is an attitude that we humans have toward things that stop us from living life to the full. Fear freezes us to the spot on the ground where we stand and prevents us from moving forward. Therefore, God does not want you or me to be restrained by fear that will cripple our lives. How can we face our fears and, with God's help, overcome them? That is the question that we can now tackle because we have already learned something of God's love and purpose for us. Once we have begun to know that there is a God and that we can have a relationship with that God, then we begin to build up confidence. We begin to trust in God's love for us and in our strength to respond to that love. We can "take our fears out of the cupboard" and examine them in the light of the gospel.

## Fears about Self

What are some of the fears that people have shared with me as we have journeyed together on our spiritual pilgrimage? They are mostly fears about self: unworthiness, lack of knowledge, need to stay in control, hidden secrets, apprehension about emotional involvement. Then there are fears about the cost of the relationship: how much time and effort might be involved, what changes in my life I might have to make, what difficulties there might be in sustaining the relationship. And, finally, there are fears about looking foolish in claiming to have a relationship with a God whose existence cannot be proved and who is regarded as unreal by so many people. As you think about this list, you may want to add one or two other fears that you have about entering into a relationship with God.

Let us examine in greater detail some of the fears that seem to occur most often. These fears may well be rooted in some feeling we possess about ourselves and about the way we relate to other people, not just to God. It is therefore important as we start to look at the list that we remind ourselves of the purpose for facing these fears. We do so because God wants a fuller life for us. God cares about our welfare. God wants us to enter into a relationship with God that is filled with mutual joy and common purpose. God does not want us to take the fears out of their hiding places to make us more frightened, but so that we can overcome them and get on with living. So what are the fears that many people have?

## Fear of Failure and Feelings of Inadequacy

Some people have a great fear of always failing in whatever they do. They are frightened that they cannot cope with situations. They fear that they have nothing to contribute to a relationship. Their lack of belief in their capabilities makes them so nervous that they often do make mistakes—say and do the "wrong" things. When they read the stories in the scriptures, they see God as relating to the "heroes and heroines," the so-called saints of the faith. So in comparison, they cannot see God choosing them as a person to whom God would want to relate. Whenever they open their mouths, they seem to put a foot in them.

At the root of such fears is an anxious self who has never been helped to find the integration of personality that allows confidence in the self to grow. All human beings make mistakes in life. We do not always make wise decisions or do what is best in a particular situation. That is part of the limitation of being human. To overcome an unbalanced view of this situation, we need people around us who will give us encouragement and help us to begin again. If we have not experienced this positive contribution from others to our growth, then of course we will have fears about failing. Jesus knew this and focused his ministry on telling people that God really cared about them in that condition. Jesus shared with them, and shares with us, that God has faith in us and gives us the Spirit to assist our recovery. Jesus called the community of disciples into being to be the mutual support group to help us overcome our feelings of failure and inadequacy. With that support we will be gently assisted to regain our confidence and make fewer and fewer "mistakes." As we learn to trust God, we learn to trust ourselves as competent and resourceful people—not totally free of failure, but always open to forgiveness and new beginnings. And the wonderful thing that Jesus taught us was that we do not have to wait until we are perfect before we can have a relationship with God. God calls each person into fellowship as they are so that they may grow into what they can be.

## Fear of Being Thought a Fool

When faced with the thought of a relationship with God, some people are afraid that they will not be able to cope with the intellectual demands of "being religious." They say they cannot understand all those theological terms. Their minds go blank when asked to explain what God is like. They think that you have to be very bright to be a Christian. They are afraid to read the Bible because it is full of such complicated language and thought. They see themselves as "simple" people. They know that God is a mystery and beyond understanding—so they are frightened of God as they are about all the things they cannot understand. They feel foolish because they cannot put into words what they mean by faith.

Such fears have little to do with a general level of education, because education hardly ever includes learning about the meaning of God. If religious education is included in our general education, it is mostly seen as "moral education"—good behavior, not a good understanding of God. As a result, many people feel ignorant about religious matters and are fearful of entering into a relationship with an "unknown" God.

Jesus seems to have been very aware of this fear that many people hold. As part of his teaching he used stories that allowed people to apply everyday occurrences to their thinking about God. Christianity is a way of living, not a set of abstract theories about God. Most Christians find that the relationship with God allows the spirit of this sort of wisdom to develop in their lives. Life, of course, is not simple, and we all know that it requires thought and care to face its complicated issues. But the relationship with God is about practical wisdom and being open to the guidance of the Spirit. Our minds are a vital part of our human bodies, and we all aim to use them to their maximum capacity. On the other hand, we should not hold back from entering more deeply into our relationship with God because we do not think we "know" enough to begin. We can let our minds explore how to communicate with God and our fellow disciples as we make progress in the relationship. The Spirit of God is the agent of such development.

**Fear of Intellectual Dishonesty**

Another fear associated with the mind is the fear of having to shut down our thinking processes in order to enter into a relationship with God. A number of people have the experience of their heart's encouraging them to develop a relationship with God and of their mind's telling them not to be so foolish. For them logic seems to rule out a relationship with a God whose existence cannot be proved. All the training they have received makes them skeptical of ideas that are not based on "facts"—the things that we can see, touch, and establish by reference to the physical world. For them everything must fit into a logical scheme to make sense. If it falls outside this scheme, it either does not count for anything or does not exist. To think clearly means that all things cohere together within this framework. For anyone with this training there is a deep fear of a relationship with God that threatens "logic" because the relationship speaks about God's initiatives of love and of the Divine breaking in upon the human. A relationship with God moves us beyond the logical structures we have created and makes us open to the previously unknown. We learn a new language created to convey the meaning of a relationship that is not confined to a limited number of definable objects. In this situation some people fear that the language used has no ultimate meaning and therefore is "meaningless."

In the face of such fears, we can take encouragement from the vast number of scholars and thinkers who have had the faith to enter into a relationship with God. Though they feared that God might be unknowable, they found the intellectual excitement of discovering that the new language they had to use for God spoke about ultimate truth—that the physical world interacted with a spiritual world that was just as "real." When we learn the language they have created, we too are helped to find the words for our similar experiences so that we can describe them to one another. At the heart of every language is a set of experiences and the words that describe those experiences. From our interaction between the happenings and the words for them we come to name certain things and thus to communicate that reality to one another. We can have full confidence that such language is of equal value to the language of any other type of experience. We will stretch our minds to bring into our widened framework a whole new set of concepts, and we will find the words to describe this. Intellectually this is what happens when we begin to think deeply about the meaning and reality of our relationship with God.

**Fear of Losing Control of My Destiny**

Some people are afraid of losing control of their thinking processes. Others fear the loss of control over their own futures. They fear that a relationship with God might wreck their careers, their set patterns of behavior, their family relationships, their sporting activities, or their choice of pleasures. They think that if they get too close to God, they will be taken over by God. They fear the loss of their ability to choose what they want to do. They think that in a relationship with God there will be a continual struggle of wills, each trying to push the other into what the other does not want. Sometimes such people have come out of a human situation where the person struggled to be free from the dominant control of another person—maybe a parent or an authority figure. Having gained their "freedom" from such a relationship, they fear that they will become the "slave" of God. The Bible's use of this word *slave* or *servant* reinforces the fear in that person. They have little experience of the mutuality of a relationship where respect and trust are the foundations of love. Many people struggle in life to gain control of every type of choice, and for them freedom has become of greater value than involvement with others. This has caused such people to hold back from entering into a relationship of any sort. Alongside a fear of the overpowering majesty of God, this fear of losing control is very strong for some people. They see the will of God not working for their best interests, but making them do things that please a God who is always imposing impossible demands. It is not the demands as such that frighten them as much as the overwhelming will of God in the face of which there is no choice left for their own decision. They fear God may overpower them.

All that we learn about God from Jesus Christ, as well as from the scriptures as a whole, is of patience, of invitation to relate, of willingness to wait for our response, and of God's unwillingness to impose God's will on an unwilling humanity. God, however, is not so disinterested in our future as to leave us without challenges. That sort of God would not be a God of love, but a God of detachment. So if there is a struggle, it is for the good of ourselves, the world community, and all of creation. The struggle is to help us recognize that our future is vital—to us and to God. We are consistently called into the relationship so that we can enjoy the presence of God and find strength for living the life that we and God together choose. God's will is for our good.

**Fear of Wasting Energy on a Trivial Matter**

There are people who think that a relationship with God would be all right, but it is of very low priority. They fear that it will take up time and energy that would be better spent on more important and rewarding matters. For them there are more important and pressing things to do in life. "Why bother," they ask, "with a relationship with God when I am fully occupied with making enough money to live on, with staying well, with working out human relationships, with making a contribution to my friends and my society?" The busy modern world seems so full of activity that people are afraid of anything that might divert them from the focused goals that they have set. It would be different if they could see "tangible" results, but a relationship with God seems so vague, and you never can be sure that it is based on reality. Things are measured in money or materials, not in faith and love.

I believe that this is a major fear in our society that holds many people back from making progress in a relationship with God. They do not feel equipped to enter into an argument about the existence of God, so that is not the issue for them. The issue is about the "importance" of everything, about the "value" of everything, about the amount of "spare time" that is left over from the most pressing of engagements.

Jesus made his hearers face up to their attitude about the importance of allocating time and energy to the things of God. He likened it to "a pearl of exquisite quality, worth a fortune." A trader in pearls would spend any effort and finance necessary to acquire such a pearl. By this saying Jesus challenged his hearers about what they considered really worthwhile in life. Those who have found the joy and fulfillment in a relationship with God tell us that it is worth dying for and certainly worth living for. A relationship with God is at the heart of our true existence and affects for good all our other activities. Such a relationship is the driving force behind all we do. Therefore, it is worth enhancing such a relationship by giving it all the time and energy that it needs.

**Fear That the Secrets of My Life Will Be Uncovered**

Shame is a major barrier for some people to a meaningful relationship with God. They are afraid that God will uncover everything that they have carefully hidden from view. Such people see in themselves a dark side that they hate. They do not want this dark side to be seen by anyone and even fear to admit to themselves that it is really there. They do not want anyone to know that at times they have feelings of hatred, of superiority over everyone else, or of lust and sexual fantasy. They even know that their dark side is capable of cheating to get their own way and of distorting the truth to show themselves to be "right." All these secrets have been suppressed and, with an inner struggle, are kept hidden from the sight of all. People certainly do not want to admit to God that they have such thoughts, feelings, and activities. They think that if they did, God would punish them for such secret thoughts and immediately break off the relationship. So they are too frightened to allow the relationship to develop. They have been taught that God forgives sins, but not sins "against the Holy Spirit," which they imagine are the secret sins of the inner mind. No one knows about them, and it would be better if God did not know about them either. So any thought of a relationship with

God is frozen at its beginning. (In scripture the sins "against the Holy Spirit" refer to those words and actions that deny that God's spirit motivated and activated the ministry of Jesus.)

When we bring such fears into the open, we can see how much they are holding us back from being an integrated self with the openness and confidence necessary for positive living. Such fears will imprison us because we will never feel free to be known and loved for who we are. We will live a lie and live in fear of being found out. Jesus clearly stated that he came to "release the captives"; to "save sinners"; to bring us all "life in abundance." Jesus was ready to share with his disciples the fact that he had inner struggles with dark thoughts. He imagined himself giving demonstrations of extraordinary power to force people to acknowledge that he was the Messiah. He told them how he could see it was possible to twist the words of scripture to prove his point. He even told them that he had thoughts of running away from the final challenge with the authorities in Jerusalem when it was clearly necessary to face up to evil and overcome it with the force of sacrificial love. If Jesus was open about his dark thoughts, why should we fear to let God know all about our outer and inner selves? The answer is that there is no point. God our Creator knows all about us and loves us fully. Humanity has been made with a complex set of thoughts and stimuli. This allows us to make responses to a variety of situations and to possess the ability to make choices. This is a key to the glory of being human, but it leaves us with the struggle to choose what is best for us and for others. To live with this struggle is to respond positively to the condition of being human. God has promised the power of the Spirit to uphold and guide us in this struggle. With this strength we can face all the thoughts and feelings we have and acknowledge them as part of us. We learn to choose what is best and set aside what is "bad." In our choosing, we name what is bad as "evil" and what brings life to us and others as "good." The evil only becomes damaging if it is declared to be good and expressed in activity. The evil also holds power over us if it is allowed to fill us with fear that it will get the upper hand in our lives. Then it cripples the good and traps us into inaction. In our relationship with God we are able to look into the whole of our lives and make the choices that are in accordance with what is best for all. We make no secret of the struggle we all have in choosing the best. We do not need to hide anything, for God sees it as part of the totality of our human nature.

## Fear That I Will Lose the Right to Be Angry and Hate Others

Most people have been hurt by others close to them at some point in their lives. Some people are afraid to enter into a relationship with God because they think that it will force them to let go of this anger and restore the relationship. Anger has been such an important part of their self-righteousness that they are frightened to let it go. Doing so may prove them to have been in the wrong. The hurts are so strong that their self-esteem is supported by this anger. It gives them a reason to maintain the broken state of the relationship. In such circumstances people fear that a relationship with God would demand that they admit they were wrong and restore the relationship. It is even possible that subsequent choices make it impossible for the relationship to be restored to where it was before. These feelings of resentment and hatred are fairly widespread in a society in which a number of types of human relationships are constantly breaking down and new ones begun. The fear of having to face up to this situation may well hold people back from developing a relationship with God. The feeling is that God would not approve of the anger and would demand restoration of the human relationships.

The truth is that such anger and resentment are not helpful to our lives and may damage our health. It will absorb the inner energies that we need to make the best choices that are possible for everyone. Anger is not bad in itself, for it is the trigger of change from depression over loss to action for a better future in new circumstances. What is bad about anger is its being allowed to persist and become a permanent state of mind. Then it is a cause of burnout. Resentment is also damaging because it denies reality. This hardness of heart stops our being open to the fullness of truth. There are always faults on all sides in the breakdown of human relationships, and these need to be acknowledged for the real situation to be faced and overcome. In a relationship with God we gain the confidence to face the truth about ourselves and about the total situation. We can then discard our resentment because we know that God's valuation of us is sufficient to build up our self-confidence, and we do not need resentment to do this in a false way. God will help us make the choices that are best for the situation. We will be given grace to forgive ourselves as well as others. Once we can overcome the fear of letting go of the resentment, we will find that our relationship with God gives us new energy to repair the damage caused by our hatred and anger.

## Fear of the Sacrifices Required in a Relationship with God

People often place great emphasis on the cost required of us to enter a relationship with God. They point out that any worthwhile activity is costly, and that it is right that the most important activity of all should be accomplished at great cost to us. They say that we can achieve nothing important without sacrifices. There is truth in this, but not when the costs are seen out of perspective. The people I speak with raise fears that it will cost a person entering a relationship with God a great amount of time, money, and the surrender of all pleasures. It will entail joining a Christian community, spending hours at prayer, giving to those in need, being nice to neighbors they dislike, taking an unpopular line about issues of race, gender, and poverty, and becoming involved with causes that touch on politics. "It is all a bit too much," some people say. They fear not the relationship itself, but the consequences in all the various areas of life. They believe that such sacrifices were easier to make when society regarded them as beneficial and they were the subject of admiration rather than ridicule. The fear arises from the current pressure on all our available resources. Most people find that they are very limited in the amount of time and money left over from the basics of living. They know that they are fragile from coping with the strains of life and have little emotional energy left for another relationship. They fear that the few pleasures that remain for them in life—a little time for themselves, a little drink occasionally, a visit to a concert or film, even a weekend away with friends—will have to be given up in the light of God's total demand. "There will be nothing left for me!" is the cry of despair.

In the face of the cross, many Christians see a call from God for total sacrifice. I am allowed to retain nothing as mine, not even my life. They see the summons as one of total commitment to which everything must be sacrificed. In contrast, the cross is God's total generosity to humanity. It is Christ who willingly makes the sacrifice for our benefit. What we give back is out of a heart that is so touched that we *want* to do whatever is best for us and for all. Nothing is extracted from us. It flows out of us, not to deprive us of what we need, but to share with God and the community what is for all to enjoy. What I give is enriched and enhanced, whether it is time, money, practical care, or words to uphold truth and justice. I may want to realign my priorities as a result of the relationship with God, but this no longer feels like a hardship; it is the cause of joy. Those who have "given things up" consider them to no longer hold the same value. When Jesus asks us to take up our cross and follow him, we are not leaving life behind, but discovering a new life of infinitely greater worth. The demands we fear are transformed through the relationship into the delights we most appreciate.

**Fear of Too Much Emotion**

Many people are afraid of emotion. They may be afraid that their emotions will cause them to do things that they will regret when they have time to think clearly. They may be afraid that they cannot maintain the emotional energy necessary to sustain a relationship in the long term. The word *love* is too emotional a word for them, and they are frightened when people use it about God. They like to keep the emotional side of their nature under control. Talk of compassion and forgiveness leaves them cold. They want to speak about justice and retribution in the face of wrongdoing. They think that God is soft on sinners and allows people to get away with murder. For them emotion distorts reality, and the heart leads people astray. They may have experienced love as blackmail: "If you love me, you will do this for me," and the "this" may be very hurtful. Such people have been burned by emotion and draw back from any relationship that talks about love. For them living is a hard reality where the head must rule the heart. Some of these people have rejected a relationship with God because they have seen or experienced so-called evangelists' working on people's emotions in a manipulative way.

Other people are frightened that they will not be able to find the emotional resources to keep the relationship with God going over a long period. They think that it might be all right at the start, but soon the heart will go out of it, and it will become a formal shell. They hold back from beginning the relationship on the grounds that they know it will not last.

The words of Jesus give proper place to emotion, but they never have any hint of sentimentality about them. They speak of love—God's love for us and our response of love to God—but the love is shown in action. It does not end in word only. It is important that we acknowledge that we need comfort and emotional support as well as physical actions to meet our basic needs. In modern society we have learned that it is not enough to throw money at a problem. We have to back it up with words of comfort, hope, and support. We have to feed the heart as well as the stomach. Our relationship with God satisfies our deepest longings and provides us with courage and a community to meet our physical needs.

### Fear of the Whole Concept of God

At the end of our list of fears we need to return to where we began in our general comments. Many people are just too frightened by the whole idea of God. For them God is too big, too powerful, too complicated, too demanding. In such a relationship the human being is always the underdog, the puppet, like a worm waiting to be picked off as soon as it struggles to the surface. The feeling is that humans are too small and God is too great for any meaningful relationship to take place. We are always left gasping for breath and can never catch up with God. The distance between us is too large. Such people are unwilling to get involved because they will never be the winners. It is not that they consider themselves too bad to enter the relationship, but they feel they can never be good enough. They will always be at a disadvantage.

Such fears overlook the experience of so many who have entered into a relationship with God. They find that they grow rather than wither in the presence of God. They tell us of the excitement of reaching their potential, which encourages them forward. They recognize what a wonderful difference the relationship has made in their lives, giving them the strength to tackle even the hardest issues. They speak of God's support and not of God's suppression. They affirm the experience of a God who walks beside them and carries them when necessary, not of a God who drags them screaming where they do not want to go.

### Your Fears

If some of those fears ring true for you, try to think of the human experiences buried in the past that may have been responsible for causing you to react with fear to the thought of a relationship with God. Here is a list of questions that may prompt you to identify those threatening situations:

Who treated you as if you were a failure?
Who told you that you were dumb?
When did you learn that logic was the way to control every situation?
With whom did you have clashes of wills?

What gave you the idea that religion and God were trivial
   things?
What caused you to hide and keep from view some of your
   thoughts and actions?
What are some of the reasons why you are angry with other
   people?
Why are you frightened of being emotional?
What makes you afraid that relationships cannot be sustained?
What have you been taught about God that makes you afraid?

## Dealing with Our Fears

Knowing that we are profoundly loved is the first step in dealing with our fears. We then make progress when we name the fears we have and, if possible, discover some of the background causes of such fears. The blockages begin to fall down as we examine our fears and get away from being afraid of being afraid. Some people still find this difficult and are frozen by fear because they know they have it but cannot identify any cause. If this is the situation for you at this time, then I encourage you to do two things:

1. Acknowledge before a loving God that you do have these fears and that you want to find a way of ridding yourself of them.
2. Seek out someone with whom you can pray and who can help you overcome these fears. Such a person might be an experienced pastor, a spiritual director, or a trained counselor. It is a sign of strength, not weakness, for someone to ask for help. It tells the other person that you are ready to do what is required and ready to receive his or her support and guidance.

Even if some fears remain, you do not have to stop reading this book at this point! However, I do pray that you will take the steps above so that you have the joy of entering freely into your relationship with God.

For those who have been able to see the causes of their own particular fears and know that they can be dealt with now, here are the steps that I suggest you take:

1. Remember that God wants you to find yourself in this relationship. God looks for your full potential. God, out of love, opens up the future for you.

2. Admit to yourself that the fears will not disappear immediately, but that their power to hold you back will fall away as you "stare them in the face." The fear of fear is the biggest hurdle.
3. Sit down with God beside you and make a list of those fears that are true for you. It is very unlikely that your list will have all the fears on it that I have outlined above. It may have some special fears of your own on it.
4. Set out a timetable for the future that will allow you to look at each of the fears in turn—maybe at the rate of one a week.
5. When you are examining the fears according to this timetable, see whether you are still afraid of that fear when you come to it. You may find the fear has gone because you have been processing the issue internally before you reached it. If it is still there, go on to ask yourself what caused the fear, and is the cause still current? Then go on to ask yourself what other experiences you have had which counterbalance that cause. See if you can draw on these experiences to work out what steps you can now take to counteract the causes of the fear. If you are having difficulty dealing with it on your own, then use the opportunity of seeking help as I have described above.
6. At the conclusion of the exercise reaffirm in prayer that God has been with you all the time, in your heart and mind, supporting you, affirming you, caring for you, forgiving you if that is what you have asked for, and reawakening in your heart the spirit of peace and hope, courage and love.

## A Prayer for the Spirit of Comfort and Truth

*God, you love us more than we can ever imagine,*
*and in Christ you have promised us peace and wholeness;*
*we look for the fulfillment of that promise*
*as we take time to face our fears.*
*Give us comfort and courage, trust and truthfulness*
*so that we can know ourselves*
*as we are fully known by you.*
*Grant us your Spirit so that we can walk securely into the future,*
*aware of your presence beside us*

*and the support of others on our journey.*
*We are bold to make this prayer,*
*for you have told us in Christ that you love us,*
*now and always.*
*Amen.*

# 4

# Worship and Affirmation

Our adoration and worship are key elements in our relationship with God. When the word *worship* is mentioned, many people think of a service in church, which, although it contains some element of praise, focuses to a large extent on teaching about God and praying for others and for our own needs. In this chapter we will concentrate on what worship means in our personal relationship with God.

## The Meaning of Worship

Worship is the activity that declares to another person how highly you value her or him in the relationship. In an old form of the *Service of Marriage* the husband said to the wife: "With my body I thee *worship*, and with all my worldly goods I thee endow." The context shows us that the word *worship* meant honor, respect, love, adore. My body would express to you that I held you in the highest place in my affections and valued you above all things. Tenderness as well as strength are implied in the word used in this context. Such "worship" would bring mutual delight to both husband and wife.

In the context of the First Testament the word *worship* is used to translate the concept of "falling down before" someone held in this highest esteem. So the subject of the sovereign worshiped the ruler, who thereby was declared to be held in highest honor. To fall down before the sovereign was to say to him: "You are the greatest—both in power and in my affections." Some people still honor the representative head of a nation with a bow or a curtsey. At its best, this is no servile action. Rather, it declares that I am delighted to be in your presence, and I acknowledge the responsibilities you exercise for the good of us all.

When we use the word in the context of our relationship with God, what do we mean by "worship"?

1. It tells God that we are delighted to be in God's presence and that it is a joy to be in this relationship with God.
2. It declares the important place that God holds in our lives. No person and no material object is more important to us than God.
3. We proclaim that God is in the first position of priority in what we value. We value God above money, leisure, status, and even our own comfort. These may have a place, but not in priority to God.
4. We offer to God the best of our thinking, our creativity, and our emotional energy. We will not do everything else first and fit God in to what is left over.
5. We show that God is the one to whom we look first of all for direction and guidance. We will not try all other avenues first and use God as a reference of last resort.
6. Our words of adoration tell God how much we love and admire God *before* there is any thought in our minds about something that we would like God to do for us.
7. By our worship of God we make clear that we are ready to listen to what God has to say to us, whether they are words of comfort or words of challenge.

## Humility and Confidence

As we come to show this worship to God, it is only natural that we are aware of our human status. We know that we can only come into this relationship because we have been invited by God to do so. We are there because Jesus has invited us to be one of God's disciples and friends. Jesus himself is our access to the presence of God. In picture language, Jesus opens the door for us and then presents us as one made worthy by his love and sacrifice. We are there not by our own right, but because Jesus has made it right for us. So we worship with humility and with confidence. We are humble because God is our Maker, our Redeemer, and our Sanctifier—that is, God who created us as human beings, through Christ renews us after failure, and by the Spirit shapes us in holiness. We are confident because God has promised to put the Holy Spirit in our hearts so that love between us and for us can grow to its fullness in unity of purpose. We are confident because Christ has claimed us as one of his own community of friends, who are partners in his works of faith and mercy.

So humility and confidence are woven together in us as we approach God in worship. Our lips will be bold to declare how much we love God and praise God for all the ways in which God is God. Our bodies will find symbolic ways to express our feelings in this act of worship. Many people have said to me that they would like help in finding ways to express what is in their hearts when they worship God. Here are two ways through which we can show and tell God of our adoration and praise:

First, we can do this through the positions we adopt for our bodies. There is a saying: "Kneel in adoration and stand in thanksgiving." When we want to express the greatness of God and the value in which we hold God, the position of kneeling to show reverence seems most appropriate. It feels right to many people to kneel in adoration. Yet as we do so, we look up with admiration and delight in our eyes, gazing upon God's majestic love for all creatures. The words of the old person with a lifetime of experience of worshiping God in quiet devotion come to mind: "I look at God, and God looks at me." There are those, of course, who find some tangible symbol of God useful at this point, be it a window, a picture, a candle, or a cross. On the other hand, it is right that we should stand in thanksgiving when we remember the status that God gives to us, as children of God and partners in the care of creation. We stand to offer to God our words of thanks for the generosity and support of God. That is also why there has been a long tradition of standing for the Great Thanksgiving prayer in the eucharist.

Second, we want to find suitable words for our lips to express to God how we are thinking and feeling. We may have the words stored up in our memories. We always want to repeat these well-known words on such an occasion. We have committed them to memory, or know where they are written down, so that our lips are not speechless in the presence of the God whom we hold in awe. This wonderful God deserves better-formed phrases than we can think up on the spur of the moment. So we have a favorite passage we repeat or a prayer of praise we know by heart.

On the other hand, there are those who want to speak directly from the heart and prefer to form fresh words each time on their lips. For them this indicates that they will never take the relationship for granted and grow cold in their affections. In these circumstances the mind will recall the ideas we want to express, and our lips will offer new phrases to tell God how much we adore and appreciate God.

**The Language for Worship**

Here are a couple of examples of each type of approach: first from scripture—one from the Psalms, which contain many passages of worship and praise, and one from Revelation, which reveals the language of "worship in heaven."

**Psalm 95:1–7**[1]

> O come, let us sing to the Lord;
> > let us shout with joy to the rock of our salvation.
> Let us come into God's presence with thanksgiving;
> > and sing to the Lord with psalms of triumph.
> For you, Lord, are a great God,
> > and a great King above all gods.
> In your hand are the depths of the earth;
> > so also are the heights of the mountains.
> The sea is yours, and you made it:
> > the dry land also, which your hands have fashioned.
> O come, let us bow down and worship:
> > let us kneel before the Lord our maker.
> For the Lord is our God,
> > we are the Lord's people,
> > > the flock that God shepherds.
> Glory to the Father, and to the Son,
> > and to the Holy Spirit;
> as it was in the beginning is now:
> > and shall be for ever. Amen.

**Revelation 7:12**

> Blessing and glory and wisdom
> and thanksgiving and honor
> and power and might
> be to our God forever and ever!
> Amen. (NRSV)

On the other hand, here is an example of words that might tumble out spontaneously from a heart full of praise and adoration of God:

---

[1] Translation from *A New Zealand Prayer Book/He Karakia Mihinare o Aotearoa* (London: Collins, 1989).

Wonderful God, I praise and adore you.
You have made me and all the world,
and in Christ you have redeemed me and all humanity.
You are great, and I hold you in highest esteem.
I love you for who you are and what you have done for me.
I will never cease to worship you, my Lord and my God.

*Silent Adoration*

I value you above all things,
and you have the place of utmost importance in my heart.
Before you I kneel in adoration
and look into your gracious face.
Your love holds me safe and keeps me in the right way.
I will rise to thank you for your abundant goodness to us all.

*A Time of Thanksgiving*

We bless you, O most holy God,
source of all life, goodness, justice, and truth.
We honor you and praise your name,
always, forever and ever.
Amen.

You may want to pause now to offer your worship to God in whatever way you see as most appropriate for you.

## Reordering Priorities

When we worship God, we express not only our love. We also reorder our priorities. We do this gladly and without grudging because we know that the new order of priorities will bring us delight and satisfaction as well as giving honor to God. When we have grown into the relationship with God, we have a new love in our lives. This has top priority for us, and we rank all our other activities in the light of this key relationship.

Some Christians feel called by God to spend all their lives uttering words of praise to God on behalf of the whole community as well as themselves. Such people "specialize" so that the words of praise are never silent. The community sets them free for this dedication and gives them the support that is required for such an endeavor. These specialists set themselves apart from the tasks of daily living, but they are not thereby made superholy. They simply express for us all by their lives how we might spend our days if we were free to do so. The choice to follow this way of honoring God will come naturally to some women and men. For them it is a joy, but it is never an easy task. It demands total concentration and dedication. Their type of worship helps us by its model and its methods. Their prayers of adoration have inspired us, and their music has caught us up in its offering of praise.

Those who worship God in the midst of the routines of life also witness to a proper way of expressing their praise and adoration. God recognizes and values the usual working/living cycle of human existence equally. The incarnation of Jesus makes this clear. We do not have to give up life in the world in order to worship God. However, we do have to reorder our priorities and review our perspectives on life in the light of our worship of God. The routines of life will still be there, and we will exercise our gifts to provide for ourselves and those who share life's journey with us. We will make a place for recreation and participate in healthy exercises, our sports, and our hobbies. We will delight in food and the occasions where food is part of fellowship. We will enter into human relationships with other people and make commitments to them. We will seek advancement in our work as a way of using our gifts more fully and providing leadership for others in the fabric of work and society.

The big change will be that none of these activities or relationships will take the place of God in our lives. Money will not make us feel superior, and status will not make us arrogant. Everything we are or do will serve our top priority of honoring God. We even know that we have to watch out for a false sense of pride that we "have done all this for God," and we must not boast to others about how we have put God first in all things. Those thoughts can undermine the whole point of worship!

The question of the use of money becomes very difficult for some people. Many feel called to give all they possess to God and even feel guilty about spending money on themselves. I suspect some dishonesty in the thought behind the line in the old hymn, "Not a mite would I withhold." Money in itself is not tainted with evil, nor do we give it away out of compulsion. As a result of our worship of God we learn to handle it effectively. It is to be used to enhance our relationships—with God, with self, and with those who share life with us in family and community. Money is not a source of status or pride, but a resource for good. From God we have learned about generosity, where the gift is used not only for the benefit of the receiver but also for the delight of the giver. No strings are attached to the gift. I do not use it to manipulate or manifest dependency. Money becomes the means of sharing. It supports those who, by misfortune, are unable to care for themselves in a society where money is the only medium by which we acquire what we need for life. In a simpler society we would do things for one another without having to use money. In a complex modern society money becomes the way of transferring my work into the means of meeting the needs of myself and others.

## New Objectives

We will find that the reranking of priorities brings delight because everything we do becomes filled with a purpose that leaves selfishness behind. All things work toward an objective—God's will—and not for our self-aggrandizement. Working has a new pleasure, and feasting has the fun of relationship rather than the fattening of the body. If we have a family, they should see a change in us as we accept and love them more fully. Our worship of God may, or may not, be shared by the other members of the family, but our own attitude toward our family members should be transformed by our adoration and worship of God. There we learn mutuality and respect and how to honor another person without any strings being attached. In every practical way our worship of God teaches us to want less for ourselves. We desire greater simplicity. We gain a clear sense of justice. We find harmony and peace, internally and externally. When we have responsibilities to others, it is important that we discuss with them any practical decisions that flow out of the reordering of our priorities. We need to be careful not to deprive others of the support they can expect from us or the time we might spend with them. Together we should decide what is best for us all. If our wish is to allocate more soul time with God, then we will put that time aside from the time we regard as "ours." We will not use up the time that we had previously shared with others in the family. There may well be adjustments that need to be made, but all those affected by them should be drawn into the final decision.

In the end, all our activity and words will become part of our worship of God. They will reflect our new priorities in life and will give glory to God. Life cannot be divided into compartments without fracturing the integration of our personality and the soul. My worship is with all my heart and soul, body, and mind; it is an offering of all that I am and all that I have and of all that I will be and do.

Up to this point, we have been looking at our worship of God and what that will mean in our lives. The flow in the relationship begins that way, but it soon develops a mutuality that brings joy to both parties. As we honor God, so we find that we are affirmed by God.

God assures us that God values the relationship and delights in our presence. We saw this affirmation in our examination of various passages of scripture. As we acknowledge God, so we hear God acknowledge us: "You are my beloved child." Jesus spoke of his disciples as his "brothers and sisters"; they were to be servants no longer, but friends. Our baptism witnesses to the new status that we acquire through our relationship with Christ. Our words of faith express our trust in God and, in return, God trusts us. This trust is shown in the way that we are called into partnership with God and equipped by the Spirit of God to fulfill our responsibilities in this relationship. To be human is to be trusted to act with God for the care of the rest of humanity and the rest of creation. When we accept the responsibility, we are empowered for our tasks by the Holy Spirit. We are given courage and grace, vision and strength, so that we can accomplish the task. The Spirit enables us to serve, and through our service we realize our value to God and to others. We do not seize status from others; we are given status because we are responsible for service.

## Values

One of the real tragedies of modern society is that the opportunity to find our value by our contribution to society is limited for so many people. The fabric of society is enhanced when all its members are involved in some way or another. By doing things with and for one another we acknowledge the importance of each member of that society. Once people begin to feel that they are totally dependent on others and have "nothing to offer" to society, then they feel not only excluded, but totally unnecessary. This may lead to attacks on society as "them," and violence in society grows. On a personal basis, it may lead to attacks on their own bodies as worthless. Such attacks may take the form of drugs, recklessness, or even suicide. Worth-ship of God can restore the proper perspective in the worshiper. There we learn again that we do matter to God; that we have gifts from God that we can share; that there is a community to which we can belong and to which we can contribute. We can never be "unemployed" if we worship God, and we can never consider ourselves as having no value if we will only gaze into the face of a gracious God.

As a result of our worship of God we place a new set of values on everything. This includes a reevaluation of ourselves as worthy of God's friendship and partnership. Our worship also helps us place new value on our fellow human beings. We see them in the light of brothers and sisters, full of potential, needing and giving support and care, and enabled by God to grow to full maturity. The mutuality and respect that we have received from God provides us with a pattern for all our relationships. In particular, we learn never to "write off" other people, but to regard them as those who are important for who they are as well as what they can "produce." With God we see the potential in their lives and encourage them to live toward that potential.

## Affirmation

Through worship we learn the importance of affirmation—affirmation of ourselves and affirmation of others. A feature of modern society is its focus on criticism. We seem to concentrate on what is wrong with every person and every situation. Then we use this ammunition to criticize those in positions of responsibility. This attitude is so widespread that it has become the predominant way of thinking in our everyday life. The first thoughts that come to mind are those of criticism and complaint. Nothing seems to be good enough, and no one lives up to our expectations. Anything less than 100 percent is seen as a failure. This has affected young people in particular. They feel that they are the subjects of constant criticism and nagging. The language used about them indicates that they are never considered good enough to satisfy our expectations. "Could do better" seems to be written on every report card. The few exceptions who are praised for their brilliance or top ability in academic or sporting achievements only heighten the sense of failure in the more average.

In this situation what is needed across the broad base of society is the sense and practice of affirmation learned through worship. Such affirmation is realistic. In worship we face up to the reality about ourselves and what we can and cannot do. We are affirmed for our progress and our potential. We are forgiven for our failures. We are encouraged toward the next goal that, with the Spirit's insight, we can see before us. We learn how to call on God to help and equip us for our tasks. Jesus teaches us how to accept ourselves as beloved of God and then to rise toward the vision of what we could be and do with God's help. We have the promise of the Holy Spirit to give us wisdom and energy for good. That is the sort of realistic affirmation that we should share with those around us, in our families, and in our communities. God is not so cruel as to make us aim at a target of the way to live without helping us acquire the skills to reach that target. Our "worth-ship" of others will be equally supportive.

I invite you to practice in your mind a few of the phrases that you would use to affirm those who are close to you. Here are a few questions you could use to stimulate your thoughts:

What do you mean when you say, "I admire you"?
What words would you use to praise others who, like us, are still imperfect?
What does it mean to say that we ought to be critical?
If you have children, how do you give them affirmation?
What should you say to those in society who are exercising responsibility?
When you have finished a task, what would you like people to say to you?
What words would you use when you want to say to someone else: "With my whole being I worship you"?

Give yourself time to practice your phrases before reading on.

## Receiving Praise

The other side of the dialogue of affirmation is the ability to receive praise and thanks. The majority of people feel good about *giving* thanks and praise to God. There is something very positive for us about that side of worship. On the other hand, there are quite a number of people who find it very hard to *receive* God's words of affirmation to them. Inwardly they feel they have never been good enough to have positive things said about them. They also think that they have so little to give that they do not deserve thanks for what they have been able to do. They are also conscious of messing things up so often that they cannot be satisfied with their achievements. So they are embarrassed by praise and thanks. They may even think that if they are not worthy of the words, then they are damned by faint praise. When affirmation comes from a human source, they may be even more embarrassed. They like to hear the words of affirmation, but they find it hard to take them on board without anxiety as to whether they are truly meant. They blush because they feel that they could never be good enough for that level of praise. They also think that it is a sign of pride to accept such words of praise and thanks too readily. Sometimes they are suspicious that the words of praise are just a prefix to the word *but...* They consider that they are simply being buttered up for the negative statement that may follow.

You too may identify with some of these feelings. We know that without affirmation our confidence withers. We know that we want the affirmation to be honest and realistic. We know that it is hard to receive praise when most of what we do is not perfect. Yet, there is much joy from hearing words that affirm what is helpful and point out what might be improved. We certainly would not wish to persist in mistakes if it were possible to put them right. Our relationship with God in worship helps us learn to receive affirmation and encouragement and to realize that realistic challenge and comfort are both necessary for our formation and maintenance as a person. We can practice giving and receiving praise in our soul time with God, and then we can act in a similar way with others, giving and receiving praise in our relationships with them.

## Attitude to Creation

There is another attitude that can change as a result of the re-evaluation that arises from our worship. This is our attitude to creation and the environment. We will see that every part of the created order is valuable to God. We will have to reconsider how we look at creation. It will no longer be there as an object for human use and abuse. Instead we will want to enter into a partnership with God in the care of creation and work toward sustaining it and in that sense "love" it. We will seek to live in mutuality and respect with all of creation. We will want to work out ways whereby humanity and the plant and animal kingdoms will live in a relationship of interdependence. We will realize that we do have a right to use plants and animals—the birds of the air, the fish of the sea, and the animals that roam the earth—as part of the food chain for human beings. Yet in that use we can never deprive the species of their right to live by taking out of creation more than is sustainable through the recovery cycle with which God has blessed it. Modern science has helped us to see the links in the chain much more clearly and has shown us the consequences of the destruction of the habitat as well as of the species. One of the difficulties for so much of humanity is that they are forced to live in a concrete environment without any contact with the earth beneath. This has hardened their hearts and cemented their minds so that they cannot understand the tenderness and wonder of the earth beneath. They are out of contact with nature for most of the time. Flowers become objects to dust, not to grow in the dust of the earth. What we do not experience directly we usually fail to understand. Spreading cities spread the disease of disregard for natural creation, and so it is treated in an unnatural fashion.

From time to time, our worship of God should take place outside as well as inside our homes, our workplaces, and even our churches. God needs to be seen in the context of creation as well as the cross. If our worship space contains the symbol of a leaf or a flower, it will help to keep the connection alive. On occasions our soul time should be taken as we walk outside in touch with the earth and sky and water. We do not worship the creation in place of the Creator, but our worship of God gives us new insight into our place in creation and the interrelationship between us and the world around us. There will be experiences of nature that help us understand more about God, and there will be experiences of God that give us new insight about how to live within the created order. Saint Francis is a model for many people in shaping a relationship with the rest of the created order. *The Canticle of the Sun* calls on the whole of creation to share with humanity the voice of praise to God:

All creatures of our God and King,
lift up your voice and with us sing;
   Alleluia, Alleluia![2]

That is an excellent hymn to use from time to time in your worship of God in order to keep you connected to all of creation, which shares with you a place in God's purposes and affections.

## Worship Shapes Life

Now that we have considered the issue more fully, we can see how widely our worship and adoration affect our lives. Life's prime purpose is to give honor and glory to God. In this we are the mouthpiece of all creation. Humanity is born to enter into this relationship with God and speak for creation in thanksgiving and praise. As we fulfill our destiny, we find that we are affirmed and given encouragement to live to the fullest. We find that we gain a realistic assessment of the way we have carried out our responsibilities as partners with God in the fulfillment of the purpose that God has for the world. We find encouragement and the confidence to see what goals we should set. We call on the Holy Spirit to give us guidance and strength to reach those goals. We reorder our priorities and see all of life in a new light. We learn to use our resources for the good of all. We gain the openness to discuss all decisions with those close to us, and we find the proper way in which to relate to them as equals in the sight of God.

---

[2]See "All Creatures of Our God and King," *Chalice Hymnal* (St. Louis: Chalice Press, 1995), no. 22.

From our experience of worship we find the words to affirm others and encourage them to reach their potential. We learn that criticism must not be used destructively, but to help us all to move on to tackle what needs to be done. We realize the importance of affirmation for children to counteract the effects of modern society.

From our experience of worship we also reevaluate our attitudes to the creation and the environment. We come to understand the concept of sustainability and the connection between each part of the creation and the rest. We learn to be in harmony with the earth and all its creatures and to join them in praise of their Creator and ours. We realize our interdependence and seek to keep more firmly in touch with the earth.

Above all, in our worship we find the words and feelings to express to God our love and adoration, staying focused to offer words of praise and affection before there is any thought of seeking things for ourselves. Our worship firmly puts God first in all things, and that brings joy to God as well as to ourselves.

I invite you to draw this chapter to a close with a prayer of thanks that you make up for yourself to express all these wonderful outcomes of your worship and adoration of God. Your concluding lines may be echoed in these words of praise:

## Praise of God

*You, O God, are my God, and I will praise you.*
*You, O God, are my Lord, and I will honor you.*
*You, O God, are wonderful, and I adore you.*
*You, O God, are supreme and holy,*
*and you have the first place in my heart.*

*For you, O God,*
*rule and reign with power and glory*
*in your kingdom of love*
*now and forever.*
*Amen.*

# 5
# Widening the Concepts of God and Ourselves

So far we have not explored to any great extent the "character" of the God to whom we are relating. What can we rightly say about this God? It is time we stretched our minds and examined a variety of images we can use to picture God.

## The Character of God

In our first chapter we noted that the Hebrews thought of God in terms of the verb *to be*. They thought of God as the One who is and was and is to come; who is ever present with us; who is powerful in all things. For them God was the great "I AM." Our *hearts* understand verbs because they evoke relationship: Your being relates to my being; your loving relates to my loving; your doing finds a response in my doing. Yet our *minds* find verbs rather hazy and prefer the definition of nouns. We like to think that

God is the Lord—whom I worship and obey.
God is the creator—who made me and all the world.
God is the conservator—who keeps the world in existence.
God is the parent—who nurtures and sees to my growth.
God is the teacher—who develops my understanding of life.
God is the guide—who sets out the signposts by which I travel.
God is the lawgiver—who sets the boundaries
   for the good of all.
God is the judge—who declares what is right and true.

The use of these personal nouns declares that we see God as the subject of a relationship that we have developed through the mutuality of our worship. Let's examine each of the nouns in turn to see how it illustrates something about the character of God.

To speak of God as *creator* is to capture something of the vastness of the being of God. When tempted to reduce God to our equal in size, it is important that we acknowledge God as Creator of the whole universe. That is the domain of God's rule. God's design is not just for me, but also for the interaction of the stars and the interrelationship of the aphids on the roses. In creation there is a delicate balance in all things. There is a power of recovery and a seed of decay. There is a diversity and a commonality. There is an equal importance of small and great. The Creator's mind lies behind all this, and the Creator's craft makes the design a reality. There is a mental and physical power behind the created order that leaves us gasping by its magnitude. In the presence of such a Creator, humanity loses any temptation to be so arrogant as to think it can be in control. Our relationship to the Creator allows us to take delight in the creation and to see ourselves working in harmony with God for the good of all.

To speak of God as *conservator* is to acknowledge that God continues to take responsibility for creation. The created order is not static, like a statue, but active and evolving. Anything living must be sustained and renewed. God the conservator continues to do that. Some people would rather use the homely word "gardener." Those with experience of that role know of the constant attention needed to assist plants to grow to their full potential. Weeds, bugs, drainage, and diseases must be seen to, and pruning, sheltering, digging, and fertilizing must be carried out to stimulate growth. The noun *conservator* includes all that activity and widens the concept to include responsibilities for planning for redevelopment and taking authority for replanting and reshaping as necessary. When we consider the parallels between this human activity and the work of God, we can meditate on the robustness and tenderness required, on the variety in creation that indicates that God must delight in all the many differences to be found in people, on the way the conservator preserves the past, but reshapes it for the developments of the future. No doubt you can think of more parallels for yourself.

To speak of God as *parent* can be confusing for some people. All of us need to acknowledge some real situations if we are to use this image to widen our concept of God. Our own parents are in a unique relationship to us. In human terms they are responsible for our existence. The actions of their bodies gave "birth" to our body. We are their offspring, and their support enabled our growth. Yet to be human meant that we also had to separate from them and find independence. Then and only then could we move into an interdependent relationship of mutual respect and delight. The struggle to achieve this goal is not without its problems and pains. Neither parent nor child is perfect, and the twists of circumstance can be tortuous. Yet all of us have some clear ideas about what that relationship *should* be like. The ideal is before us even if the reality does not always fully attain it. To speak of God as parent is to use the ideal rather than the projection of the limited reality. We do not make our parent into God or God into our parent! Yet the noun is helpful when applied to God because it describes the tasks of nurture, care, protection, love, stimulation, challenge, provision, and training that parents do for their children. Above all, it is the intimacy within the relationship that draws us to see how suitable the word *parent* is for God. Jesus summed it up in the use of "Abba" to speak to God as parent and in his description of a mother hen and her chickens. The word *Abba* is translated "my father," and this male parent description of God has predominated in liturgical usage for many years. As God can never be restricted to the gender terms of male and female, it has become the custom among some Christians to lessen the use of "Father" for God, and to think of a personal God in the roles of the more inclusive word "Parent." In such a God we look for affection without sexuality, for criticism without condemnation, for a bond of love that can be denied, but never broken. We look for all those things that, in the ideal, the parent can do for the child to bring about maturity, which is the goal from birth.

The role of *teacher* in some cultures has been fulfilled by parents, but in others it has been carried out by those appointed by the wider community to transmit its corporate wisdom. We are all fortunate that as individuals we are not required to gather all information from our own research and experience. There are teachers to translate and transmit knowledge to us so that we can make it our own. For the Hebrew people the "rabbi" or teacher was a key member of the community, and the synagogue was the place of learning as well as worship. To speak of God as teacher is to recognize that God is the source of all knowledge and that God translates and transmits to us what we need to know about our world and how to live in it. God reveals to us what we should know and does not hide from us the knowledge that makes sense of life. Through learning we discover the wisdom that makes the world the place it is. God the teacher wants us to gain that knowledge for the good of all. As partners of God, we too become teachers of what we have learned, passing it on with excitement and generosity, for it is not ours to retain. Knowledge belongs to God and God's community and is to be freely shared among all.

To speak of God as *guide* is to use a metaphor that travelers understand very well. For a sea voyage the image will be that of a pilot who steers the ship through difficult waters and brings it safely to its haven. For land travel the image will be of the guide who knows how to avoid the dangers and instead points out places of delight and nourishment. When we speak of God as guide we see ourselves trusting God to show us the pathway to reach our destination of maturity. In modern life, abundant choices are before us. This is confusing as well as exciting. Some people long for a straightforward world where choices are more limited and the responsibility of making the right choices is less onerous. The demand for guidance in society is strong. A good guide can support me as I make the hard choices and help me understand the issues with patience, without taking away my responsibility. In our soul time we will be able to picture God as guide, able to warn us of the dangers and to point us in the direction of life in its fullness. The guidance of God has been distilled over the years so that the scriptures and the tradition of the church have recorded the signposts and the danger signs for us. Our times of meditation allow God to be our guide as we use mind and heart to be in touch with God.

To speak of God as *lawgiver* is to challenge the idea that we as humans can make up the rules by which we live. The lawgiver defines the boundaries for the community so that common life is possible. God designed the boundaries within which the created order must operate. To break the boundaries is to cause damage to the parts and to the whole. The same principle lies behind living in community. The Hebrews saw God as lawgiver for their community, declaring ten firm principles by which they must live. These were there to develop positive attitudes about living together in harmony—common worship, common rest, common respect—and to set boundaries against negative behavior: perverting God's power, using violence, abusing relationships, breaking the bonds of fellowship by stealing goods or reputations, or arousing lust or greed. Throughout scripture the lawgiver God is seen as defining the positive and negative attitudes required for living in relationship with God and the rest of humanity. To fail to live up to these rules of behavior is to threaten the life of the community at every level, from the family to the world, and to damage the fabric of that society. The evidence of the effects of the failure is clear, but humanity in its innate selfishness finds it hard to give up the notion that each individual is free to define his or her own boundaries. To acknowledge God as lawgiver leads to harmony and wholeness for ourselves and for our universe.

To speak of God as *judge* is only frightening for us when we ignore the main purpose of having judges, that is, to uphold justice in society as a whole rather than simply to hand out punishment to the individual. We need a God who will make clear for us what is right and true in each situation. The perversion of justice is the biggest threat to any society and therefore to all individuals within it. We feel the outrage when a justice system fails to declare the criminal guilty and denies the rights of the innocent and the harassed. This is the proper moral reaction to injustice. People have called on God to act as judge in society to keep the powerful from using wickedness to achieve their ends and to protect the innocent from condemnation and corruption. The good judge upholds the law by making it clear and applying it to the situation at hand and by imposing the application of the law on the people concerned. Because of our own sense of wickedness, on occasion we can be frightened to contemplate God as judge. Yet the judge is both just and merciful, and forgiveness is possible as long as we do not confuse goodness and evil, right and wrong. Therefore, we can never say "we have no sin" without committing the more terrible of sins. When we confess our sins, both justice and mercy are possible, for we are facing reality and declaring where goodness and evil lie.[1]

## The Character of Christ

Humanity's concepts of God were broadened and "brought down to earth" in the life and witness of Jesus Christ. From the pages of the New Testament we can see Jesus acting in all the roles in the list above. His teaching gives us food for thought about the importance of understanding the nature of God. Jesus' memorable stories illustrate many of these concepts and help them sink deeply into our consciousness. Look out for them when you are reading your Bible.

The four gospels also record for us the range of emotions that Jesus showed in various situations. Jesus, as God incarnate, helps us to understand the heart of God as well as the mind of God. As we

---

[1] We will look at these issues more fully in chapter 9.

seek to be in touch in our relationship with the whole of God, it is time to look at the emotions recorded in the gospels. There in Jesus we find the whole range of emotions that belong to humanity: pleasure, joy, love, and hope; anger, sadness, and apprehension.

Jesus shows *pleasure* as the seventy disciples' mission to spread the good news about Jesus comes to a successful conclusion (Lk. 10:17–20). They return in joy, and Jesus affirms their power to overcome evil; he warns them of overconfidence and then with pleasure assures them that their "names are written in heaven" (meaning that they are part of God's great company of the faithful). Here we see the delight and warmth in the heart of God when things go well: The gospel is preached, and men and women are faithful to the call of God. Such pleasure is reflected in Christ's words, "It is your Father's good pleasure to give you the kingdom" (Lk. 12:32).

Jesus shows *joy* in his words to the disciples at the Last Supper. He wants his disciples to share the joy that he has found in his close relationship with the Father. He wants them to dwell in God's love "that my joy may be in you, and that your joy may be complete" (Jn. 15:11). This passage portrays the unity of love within the Godhead and tells how it brings true joy that can be shared by those who, through Christ, dwell in the presence of God. The message is so important that it is repeated as part of Jesus' prayer to God for his disciples: "I speak these things in the world so that they have my joy made complete in themselves" (Jn. 17:13). Joy is obviously part of the emotions within the heart of God that Jesus reveals to us.

John's gospel also depicts Jesus expressing the emotion of *hope*. This is a confidence in God's power even in the midst of tragedy. Jesus shows us a deep sense of trust that the power of God will always be used for the good of people. Despite the evil surrounding him, Jesus was no pessimist. He was sure that the power of goodness and love would win. This is an important aspect of Jesus' teaching and living that we need to grasp. Even in the face of the death of Lazarus, his dear friend, he is able to say to Martha: "Did I not tell you that if you believed, you would see the glory of God?" (Jn. 11:40). Thus he shares with Martha his own hope and trust in God's goodness and love.

On many occasions Jesus shows us the strongest emotion of all—that of *love*. It has become so central to our understanding of God that one of the epistle writers can declare: "God *is* love" (1 Jn. 4:8). Such love is embodied in the life and actions of Jesus. Jesus loves Martha, Mary, and Lazarus (Jn. 11:5). Jesus loved the disciples as his own (Jn. 13:1). Even at the point of death, Jesus loves his mother and his friend so much that he commits them to the care of each other (Jn. 19:26–27). Jesus declared that love was to be found in the sacrifice of one's life for one's friends (Jn. 15:13). The disciples were to abide in his love (Jn. 15:9). The emotion of love is the strongest because it endures all attempts to break it. In this sense, we can think of God as totally reliable, unshakable, and unchanging in devotion to us and all the created order. "O Love that will not let me go" expressed in the hymn the depth of assurance that that kind of strong love is at the very heart of God.

At this point in the chapter you might like to break off your reading and turn to your Bible to read that wonderful passage about love that you will find in 1 John 4:7–12.

## The Full Range of Emotions

We need to remember that Jesus showed us another set of emotions as well as those above. It is important that we consider these to gain the broader picture. The other side of love is *anger*. This should be shown when we are faced with the sight of people hurting one another and themselves. There are two examples of how Jesus showed anger in Saint Mark's gospel. First, early in his ministry, Jesus attempted to cure a man with a withered arm on the sabbath day in the synagogue. When he did so, he was condemned by those who said he was breaking the law of God about the Sabbath. Mark records that Jesus "looked around at them with anger; he was grieved at their hardness of heart" (Mk. 3:5). Jesus knew that the pain of the man was more than enough and there was no need to add to it by the condemnation of those who presumed to know what God considered most important. Jesus' anger was not for himself, but for the pain that one group of human beings was inflicting on another in the name of God. The same motive is behind his actions of anger in driving the traders out of the temple (Mk. 11:15). They were making it impossible for one group of people to use the space allotted to them for worship. The traders may also have been dishonest in the prices they charged for the animals for sacrifice. In anger Jesus flings over the money tables and drives out the traders. The anger is over the injustice and the pain that one group inflicted on the other.

The sight of human folly not only made Jesus angry but also moved him to tears of *sadness*. As Jesus approached the city of Jerusalem for the last time, he "saw the city [and] wept over it" (Lk. 19:41). Jesus knew of the potential of Jerusalem to be an example of a people true to God in worship and living. He was very aware that this potential had not been fulfilled because of jealousy, avarice, conflicting views about God, stands over tactics, and struggles by individuals for power. The city of peace was controlled by violence, and the city of God would reject God's own Son. No wonder Jesus wept.

Jesus also wept at the tragedy of human suffering and death. When Lazarus died, Jesus shared the tears of the family and friends (Jn. 11:35). There was an empathy with humanity when the struggle of life seemed to be snuffed out. Jesus' tears gave sympathy, but he also gave an assurance that in God's plan death is not the end—resurrection to eternal life is. In the face of death we weep together, and we believe together that immortality shall overcome mortality and that death cannot separate us from the relationship of love with God.

Such belief did not leave Jesus untouched by the emotions of *fear* and *apprehension*. As one who was fully human as we are, Jesus shared with us the question, "What if?" He could be troubled in spirit at the thought of death: "Now my soul is troubled." Here we see Jesus in that state of apprehension about the future that does not deny faith, but knows that uncertainty is part of human existence. I can be certain of God's love and still be afraid that in the crisis I will forget it and try to escape rather than stand up for what is right. Does this emotional reaction of Jesus only belong to his humanity? For the most part, yes. Yet I can also see that in part it is true of God. God's faith in us must be sorely tested on many occasions. It is not hard to imagine God wanting to turn away and leave us in our own mess. Faith that human sin will not be the last word must be just that for God as well as us—faith rather than certainty. For faith can only be exercised in uncertainty. Fear and apprehension are the backdrop of faith. In this sense, I can see God sharing the emotion of apprehension as Jesus did. This is a good point at which to pause and pray:

## A Prayer of Love

*Lord Jesus, you shared fully in our humanity,*
  *that you might reveal to us the heart and mind of God.*
*We delight in the pleasure, joy, hope, and love you share with us,*
  *your friends.*
*We feel with you in your times of anger, sadness,*
  *and apprehension.*

*Bind our hearts together so that in our relationship of love
we can know you more fully and express before you all our
  emotions,
for you understand us and all our needs, now and always. Amen.*

## The Character of the Holy Spirit

A focus on the Holy Spirit can also help us widen our concept of God. We experience this way of knowing God more fully as we live out our lives in faith. When we do that, we find that the Spirit of God can be described as an *energy* and a *life force* that enables us to put into practice the goals we have set for ourselves under the guidance of God. It is no wonder that the writers of scripture used the word "breath" to describe the energy that comes from the Spirit of God. They found that the "breath" of the Spirit gave them power for the race through life similar to the power the breath in their lungs gave them for the race on the track or hill. Such a Spirit was exhilarating and energizing. It gave them insight into the energy of God to sustain the creation and the enthusiasm of God to bring all of humanity into harmony.

Such a Spirit also allowed them to share in the *joy* that we saw was a mark of the life of the incarnate Christ. This joy of the Spirit was experienced as rather overwhelming in its zest for life and its confidence and boldness in the face of opposition. It was remarkable in every way. When the disciples and the fellowship of the growing church met together, they found that this joy of the Spirit reached deep down into their souls and transformed their restricted lives with a new joy of freedom. Burdens and yokes were lifted from their shoulders, and they recognized how the pervading joy of the Spirit had entered into their fellowship.

This experience of joy so bound them together that they reached out to one another in their differences with a *love* that united them. As they had heard Jesus speak of love and had watched him live by that deep emotion of the heart, so the disciples spoke of the way that the Spirit as love possessed their hearts and empowered their relationships. Slave and free, Jew and Gentile, women and men learned to respect one another through this love, and it showed in their unity and common actions. Some of the old jealousies were challenged and disappeared under the power of the Spirit. The Spirit's power allowed the gospel to leap over the old boundaries of race and culture. The followers of Jesus had to face the fact that the brothers and sisters in the faith brought with them many different languages and customs. The challenge was to overcome the entrenched attitudes with a new kind of love that made old enemies into new friends. This could only happen when the Spirit of love put a new heart into them all and allowed them to see the other as part of "us" and not "them." The circle of love widened and grew till it embraced all peoples.

The journey of life for these disciples, as it is for us, was never smooth. The explosion of the gospel leaves many bits to be tidied up afterward. Yet in these trials of opposition and confusion, they experienced the Spirit as the source of *peace* and *patience*. Such a peace gathered all into a coherence around faith and trust in God. The Spirit brought inner peace despite some outward storms, for it always kept the presence of God vivid for the believer. The disciple through the Spirit was enfolded in the care of God. The Spirit could be trusted to give guidance and the power to fulfill the purpose of God. The Spirit's patience was founded on hope. Hope allowed waiting to be a sign of confidence rather than frustration. We do not find any sense of panic with God, for there is such a hold on the present that the future can be allowed to unfold. In this we believe that there will always be a further response of divine love for the situation.

## Our Character

Having widened our concept of God, we are encouraged to widen the concept of who we are and what we can become. Transformed by such a Spirit, we begin to have a concept of ourselves where the possibilities for growth abound. We no longer feel hemmed in by the events of the past or by fears for the future. Inspired by the Spirit, we can lift our horizons and ask ourselves some searching questions:

How can I grow?
What dreams and hopes do I have for the future?
What role can I play in partnership with God?
How will I know how to claim that I am a "mature" Christian?

*Growth* will take place as we stretch the boundaries of our thinking and doing and allow God to inspire and enable us. A plant needs to face the sunlight for growth to occur. We need to face God with confidence and hope as we allow ourselves to grow in understanding and Christian action. In this chapter we have described God as guide and teacher. We must open our minds to learn from God new things that we never thought possible. We must open our hearts, expecting that God will fill us with breath to do new and exciting things in the name of Jesus Christ. As we take stronger steps, we will look for the signposts and the danger signs, but the peace of God will give us the strength and patience, yes, and perseverance, to keep going. We will move out to the "growing edges" where the real action takes place, whether in thought or in practical matters.

*Dreaming* is an exciting exercise when it is coupled with praying. It allows us to "float free" from the enclosures that we have built around ourselves in our insecurity. Once we have given ourselves permission to dream, we will find that we gain a new freedom. The quality of hope then allows us to test our dreams with the reality that God inspires. Hope never dashes our dreams, but it does allow us to "wake up" and see them from the perspective of reality and of our knowledge of God. Then we will be able, with confidence, to delete those parts of our dream that are just wishful thinking and entail no effort on our part. Hope allows us to test the dream with such questions as: Why would you want this to happen? Who would benefit if this dream came true?

Hope will help us hang on to those parts of the dream that we can fulfill in the new strength that God gives. When our dreams have been fine-tuned by hope, we are ready to ask ourselves what role we have to play in partnership with God for the reshaped dream to come true. What we hope for, we must be ready to work for! We are partners in God's world, not passengers or spectators. To be a partner with God is to be endowed with gifts that will bring to fulfillment what we know from God's guidance is good for us and for all around us. Such a partnership transforms the situation. It is out of the experience of working with God that we find out what is best, what is possible, and what is impossible or even detrimental. As we put our faith into action more and more, we get the measure of our dreams. We gain both in confidence and the wisdom of reality. Yes, we are moving toward maturity.

## Maturity

As mature Christians, we will have such a knowledge of God and of ourselves that we can look at each issue and apply the principles gained from our experience and that of others. These, with God's help, will guide us to make the right response. In our maturity we will know how to pray, discern, plan, draw strength from God, and measure success. Let's look briefly at each of those statements in turn.

*Mature prayer* allows us to focus on God before we focus on the issues that face us. We will remind ourselves of the nature of God and the abundant love that God has for us. We will fortify our hope and gain the encouragement we need to think and act for the good of all. We will take time to be still in the presence of God so that our minds and emotions are at peace. We will keep our eyes fixed on God and God's will for humanity. We will not panic before the storm or become overexcited at the thought of success. In confidence and strength we will be settled and grounded in the faith. These are the characteristics of mature prayer.

As mature Christians, we will have the gift of *discernment* that comes from God and from our experiences in the past. We will be able to measure the situation against the mind of Christ as revealed in scripture. We will recognize the prompting of the Spirit. We will be able to lay out the situation, to define the opportunities and the dangers. We will seek the opinions of others whom we trust. We will converse with God about the situation in prayer and use the gifts of the mind that have been given to us. We may even want to write down our response to check it out for ourselves before we make the final decision. When we have reached this point we will commend it to God in prayer.

After we reach a decision, it is time to move on to work out a *plan of action.* In this we will know that we are partners with God and with all those who will share the tasks with us. Our planning will draw on the input of others and the logic that comes from training. We will resist impulse and use the patience that the Spirit gives. Each task will be defined and assigned. We will exercise the unity of the Spirit that builds up the team.

When the plan is formed, we will gather all involved around us to *wait upon God* in prayer, knowing that we need God's strength to do God's work. We will not expect the miracle of magic, but the deep energy that God has promised to those who draw breath from the Spirit. In our gathering we may use the outward symbols of the laying on of hands or even anointing. We will know that the strength of God will not fade, but that it will be renewed through constant prayer as each hurdle is faced and surmounted.

When the work is complete, the mature Christian will know how to *measure success.* We will share in the joy of God over what has been achieved and in the joy that comes from forgiveness for the failures that are in every task. We will give the glory to God, and we will be ready to hear God's message: "Well done, thou good and faithful servant." (Mt. 25:21, KJV). We will measure success more in terms of faithfulness than victory. We will be cautious both of pride and false modesty. We will allow others to thank and praise us, and we in turn will offer thanks to those to whom we relate. With the maturity of old friends, each knowing the part to play and each sharing in the other's rejoicing, we will share fully our feelings and findings with God. Maturity comes when we can smile at the past, the present, and the future with quiet satisfaction and full adoration of God.

It is time to end this chapter with a short prayer of thanksgiving:

## A Prayer of Thanksgiving

*God of infinite goodness and wisdom,*
  *we thank you for all the insights that we have been given.*
*Help us to live on the growing edges of our knowledge of you*
  *and of ourselves.*
*Give us courage to move forward and new experiences to explore.*
*Equip us for the tasks that face us*
  *and inspire us with your Holy Spirit.*
*In success and in failure bring us back to yourself*
  *for thanksgiving and forgiveness,*
  *and may we share the joy of your heart in both.*
*This we ask as servants and partners of Jesus Christ,*
  *your Son and our Lord.*
*Amen.*

# 6

# Coping with the Storms in Life

### Storms on the Sea of Galilee

On a visit to Israel some years ago, my wife and I took a boat from Tiberias to a pier near Capernaum across the Sea of Galilee. We started out on a sunny, calm afternoon, but when we were about halfway across, the wind suddenly rose, and the sun was hidden by threatening clouds. We were shocked that the waves could form so quickly as the wind gathered speed down the funnels of the hills surrounding the lake. Our boat was high in the water, and the storm passed over quickly, but it was an experience that we will not forget. For a time fear had replaced pleasure, and apprehension took the place of appreciation.

That incident helped us to read about the storm on the lake in Mark's gospel in a new light. You will find it in chapter 4, verses 35 to the end. This story tells of a storm on the lake and of the disciples' faith that Jesus was in control of every situation. I am sure that incident was remembered because it applied to the "storms in life" as well as the storms of nature. Storms in life are those occasions when external or internal forces threaten to overpower us, and we fear that we will lose our grip on ourselves. This may occur when we suffer major losses, when we have a flare-up in human relationships, when accidents happen, when open or subtle persecution hits us, when we have a turmoil in our faith. A common feature of these storms in life is that in them we feel cut adrift from our anchor and fear that everything we hold dear will be swept away. We may even fear that we may die.

## The Storms of Life

In the storms of life, the emotions run riot, and our physical bodies may be seriously affected. Panic may set in, and we may not be able to think clearly. The major feature is that we feel "out of control." The external forces are so strong that we do not believe we can make appropriate responses anymore. It feels as if we are swimming in a strong current that threatens to sweep us away, no matter how hard we swim. Pause for a moment and try to think of occasions when you had those types of feelings. Then ask yourself what you did and what you now see that you could have done when the storm hit you.

Let's return to the Bible passage to use the image of the storm to point out some key principles for Christians as they cope with the storms of life.

### Learning from the Bible Story

First, we should note that frequent travelers on the Galilean lake, and certainly all who made their living by fishing on it, were aware that storms will, from time to time, race down from the hills. They are part of the known forces of God's creation. Storms are going to come, and those who sail on the lake have to be ready for them. So it is in life. We will be caught out all the more if we pretend that life will be free from storms. No one looks for them or enjoys them, but it is unlikely that we can avoid them. It is also unhelpful to say that it is God who causes them. Storms represent the hazards of human existence, and to live, we have to accept that this is a risky world. God has given us the ability to manage the risks and promises us that nothing at all can separate us from God's love. That is our "storm anchor."

Reading the account in Mark's gospel, many people feel angry that Jesus stays asleep on a cushion in the back of the boat when the storm is at its height. They feel that it is a sign that God does not care when we are in great difficulty. That was neither true in the real situation facing Jesus and his friends on the lake nor in God's reaction when we are facing the storms of life. The truth was that Jesus was a carpenter from the inland town of Nazareth, and his friends were experienced fisherfolk from the lakeside village of Capernaum. Sailors are the most experienced people in a storm. Jesus lay there having complete faith in their skill to handle a difficult situation on the sea. But they panicked. They lost faith in God and in their own skills. Jesus lost neither. He had an inner peace that he transmitted to them and to the whole situation. Jesus knew that such storms pass and that

God's grace would be sufficient for them all. In fact, it was more important for his friends to hear the word of peace than for the elements. On that lake, storms come quickly and also go quickly, dangerous as they are while they last. If it had been a different type of long-lasting storm, no sailor would have agreed to use the boat. They were good judges of the weather. And the story makes clear that there was a small fleet of boats crossing together, so the common decision must have been that the weather looked safe enough to cross the lake.

The storms of life are common to many people. They come and they go. They are part of life. God has promised us grace to help us use our skills to ride out the storm until the calm returns, and then we can continue the journey. As Jesus said, faith is required. We must have faith in God's continuing love and care, and faith in our own ability to come through the experience. Human capability and divine grace go hand in hand.

**Coping with Panic**

Our second area of learning is how to cope with panic. Obviously, that is the important issue for us all when the storms of life hit us. Here are some ideas expressed in the language of the sea that people have shared with me over the years:

1. Trim the sails; that is to say, do not attempt to do anything more than is absolutely necessary while it storms. All our energies will be required to weather the storm.
2. Keep the boat facing into the waves; that is to say, face the situation squarely. Do not try to turn and run away. Do not go "side on," chasing side issues that have nothing to do with the main problems or causes.
3. Put out the storm anchor; that is, dig deep into your faith in God and the assurance of God's love.
4. Recall the skills that you have practiced from the past: how to pray, how to discern God's guidance, how to think out the best response.
5. Use the team of others in the boat; that is, encourage and call on the strengths and skills of one another. You do not have to cope alone.
6. Exercise the patience and perseverance of the Spirit. Keep telling yourself that, with time and care, the storm will subside, and your life can go on.
7. Stop the body's racing and take time for rest periods.

### Where Is God?

The third point is, how do we deal with our question, Where is God in all of this? Usually the answer is—the subject of our blame! When the storm hits, we often become angry and project our fear onto others and very often onto God. With the sailors in Mark's story, we shout at God and say: "Don't you *care* that we are perishing?" We want to make God responsible for the crisis. We want to protest the seeming lack of God's care. We want to blame God for letting it happen. If you were Jesus in the storm, how would you have answered the question? I can imagine this answer: "Of course I care. I have faith in God and in you. Don't panic, the storm will pass, and if you regain your inner peace, so will creation. Listen, God's peace is for you and for creation. Peace, be still."

In our life-storms we need to draw deeply on the reassurance of God's love. Unfortunately, we tend to think that God must be sleeping or uncaring whenever anything bad happens to us. We so quickly forget that we live under the sign of the cross—the sign of pain and love interwoven into resurrection. God's care is most active in the crisis, at the crossroads, when life is tough and confusion confounds. Jesus helps us control our hearts with the words: "Peace, be still. My purpose for you and the world is unshakable. Nothing, yes nothing, can separate you from God's love." Let those words sink into your heart and mind before reading on.

So that we can be better prepared for the storms of life, we need to examine some of the causes and give some examples.

### Causes of the Storm

The basic feeling during such crises is a sense of losing control of our lives. The cause for this may be physical—some sickness, accident, or breakdown. The cause may be emotional—a collapse in relationship, an argument, the death of someone we love. The cause may be external—a failure of a business venture, being laid off, or other loss of income. The situation may be one of our own making or someone else's, or something else may be responsible for it. Whatever it is, at the root of the trouble is this feeling that everything is out of control.

Our first reaction may be shock and disbelief, and we try to pretend that the situation does not exist. In this phase, it is very important that we take the situation to God in prayer. This will help us to regain reassurance and reality. We will again remind ourselves of God's love and then face the reality of the situation. We need to define both the situation and the cause. There is a temptation to exaggerate or to underestimate the difficulties. It is good to have a partner in prayer to help us at this point. Our partner (and God) can assist us to "take a compass bearing" to see what the real issues are.

Our second reaction may be to "thrash around in the water" and use up a lot of energy in the struggle for survival. We have to concentrate our energies on the main issue and formulate a plan before we try to rush off and fix everything. We need to ask ourselves: What can I do that will really make a difference in the situation? Which causes can I correct, and which causes are irreversible? We need to identify our options and work out our priorities for action. Talking them over with God and our friends is always important.

Our third reaction is probably to see hope appearing on the horizon. The storm is certainly still real, but we come to see that there is every likelihood that it will pass and that the situation can be improved. Some little things usually stimulate hope—a flower blossoming in the garden, a phone call from a friend, a success in a small step taken, faith that our prayer has been heard by God, a verse that stands out for us in our scripture reading, or even a good night's sleep, which is a sign that we have relaxed a little.

Despite what I have just said, the fourth reaction might well be despair. We thought that an improvement was on the way and, crash, we are down to rock bottom again. The storm usually lasts for longer than one episode, and we have to have the gift of perseverance to see it through to the end. Many folk bear witness to the need for a team of people to pray at this point, people who also put their skills at the disposal of the one hit by the storm. If it happens that others succeed in making a difference, and we feel that we have failed, then we need to be careful of dejected jealousy. The important thing in a storm is that we all come through it to begin life again. It does not matter who keeps the boat afloat!

## New Confidence

The final reaction should be one of new confidence—a new faith in God and in ourselves—gained from seeing the situation return to some normality to which we can respond. It always takes time and prayer as well as plans and action to reach this point. At the end of that particular storm in life we should be stronger in every way. When any of us recovers from loss, we have an experience that moves us into a new level of capability to respond to life: firmer in our faith in God and stronger in the skills we have acquired. We will have learned the importance of friends. We will know deep inside that when the next storm comes, we will not panic quite as much.

## Learning from the Small Storms

As we build up experience from each time of testing in our lives, it is important that we make use of situations we would describe as "small storms" to gain the skills to deal with the bigger issues when they come. For young people, the experience of "saying good-bye" is often painful, and therefore they avoid it. But one day they will have to leave home, and will need experiences of dealing with their feelings in small losses prepare them for the trauma of this bigger loss. To cope with the pain of leaving home will in turn prepare them for the time when they have to face the loss of a dearly loved person. At one time it was thought best to exclude children from funeral services except in the tragic circumstances of the loss of a parent or sibling. Now we are wiser and see that it is much more helpful to prepare our children for any major loss by including them with the adults in the circle of those who attend a funeral. The same principle of preparation is true in dealing with our experiences of failure. We should learn from our small failures so that we are better equipped to face times of significant failure later on. We often try to excuse our failures and escape the consequences. So we learn little to prepare us for the failures and breakdowns that cause major storms later.

Try to use the opportunities that come your way in small situations so that you become skilled at coping with the larger issues. It is good to use some soul time to identify how you felt, how you prayed, what skills you discovered were valuable in the situation, and what use you made of your friends.

## Recovery

One of the greatest temptations when we are faced with a storm in life is to pretend that it is God's responsibility to fix it. The story in Mark's gospel can mislead us at this point. It is important to look at it again and to see that it is part of a sequence used by the author to reveal who God is and how God acts. It is true that Jesus is part of the action that saves the situation. But we need to read Mark 5:1: "They came to the other side of the sea." Even though we know that the author of Mark's gospel had no intention of writing a verbatim record of events and chose those parts of the story that best illustrated his message, there is still a sense of connection between each passage. We do not always see this because we read the Bible in small sections.

For Mark, the calming of the storm on the sea is a prelude to the calming of the storm in the life of a man in chaos through possession by "Legion." Both stories illustrate the peace that Jesus came to bring. These two incidents are connected in Mark's gospel by the sentence "They came to the other side of the sea."

What the sentence tells us is that the sailors had their work to do in recovering from the storm. The recovery was a partnership where God and humanity worked together. That is the way we come through all our storms. We need to use God's grace that is freely made available for us. We need to use our natural skills and the skills we have built up through experience. There will be times when we realize that God had to take a major role in seeing us through a particular storm. We may have felt extra strength from on high, or had the intervention of a Christian friend, or experienced a profound peace that took away all our fear. But God always works with us and not in place of us. We may be carried for a while, but it is not God's intention (neither should it be our wish) to cause us to revert to the dependency of childhood. As soon as we can, we will want to take up the journey again. We will feel uncomfortable if we are carried for longer than is absolutely necessary. We are always encouraged to sail on to "the next port of call" or, to use Mark's words, "the other side of the sea." That point is well illustrated by the ending of the account of the healing of the man in the chaos of possession. He was reclothed and in his right mind. His peace had been restored. When Jesus was about to climb back into the boat, the man wanted to go with him. He wanted the security of being with Jesus. However, Jesus refused and told him to go home to his friends. The man had to return to the normality of life to show that the storm was over and to pick up the thread of living. That could have been the moment for another panic, but the man understood how he had to play his part in the restoration. He went on his way and told his story with such enthusiasm that everyone realized that, through the grace of God, the storm was over and his life had blossomed. God and humanity had worked together to achieve this amazing result.

## Preparation and Resources

There are a number of ways that we can assemble the resources to be ready when the storm hits us. It will be helpful to have them in place so that during the emergency we know where to find them and how to use them. One of the difficulties in any crisis is that our minds are numbed by the shock. We are built this way to stop us from collapsing altogether. The numbness gives us time to come to terms with the difficulties and to respond to them as best we can. It is as the numbness wears off that panic can set in and freeze our minds so that we cannot act. At that point, prepared routines are very valuable because they use less energy than anything that we do for the first time. We need to save our energy to deal with the most pressing tasks before us.

I have found three kinds of resources that are very helpful to have on hand for the time of crisis. They all bring peace to the soul, clarity to the mind, and support to the faith. Such resources fall into these categories:

- Music
- Scripture
- Prayer

Of course, they can all be combined for use with one another, but for the sake of clarity, I will refer to each under its own heading.

## Music

Many different kinds of music can provide a deep anchor for the soul in a time of crisis. Music will draw me out of the whirlpool and steady my soul. We all have our favorite pieces and our favorite styles of music. For our purpose, we need to have previous experience of the way these pieces of music can calm and support us. Some like words and music, and some the music alone. Some who are musical wish to play the piece themselves, while the majority are happier with the music recorded for them on a CD or tape. When we hear music that does something special for us—reminds us of God's presence, restores our sense of harmony, helps the soul be in touch with our feelings, recalls past events that give us hope and courage—then we should note it in a place easily found for use in a time of crisis. Our ears will transmit to our brains the sense of design and purpose in the music, helping us see that there is a design and purpose in all of life. In our times of confusion and turmoil, there will be music that resolves itself like the calm after the storm. When we have notes to accompany words that express feelings of hope in the face of dismay, courage in the face of crisis, and healing through the grace of God, then the words and the music will reinforce each other and speak deeply to us. When you have finished reading this chapter, you might like to make a list of at least three pieces of music that you have identified as matching the requirements that I have just outlined. I suggest that you choose at least one piece of music alone and one piece with suitable words and music.

Many of us have found the music from the Taizé Community in France excellent for meditation in times of crisis. The rise and fall of the chant and the focus on a few key thoughts seem to calm the spirit. Because the chants are used repetitively, the words sink deeply into our consciousness and reinforce our faith in God and in ourselves. Such music can create those sparks of hope I spoke of earlier. This book does not include music notation, so I can only quote the words of the Taizé chants I have found suitable. These examples will help you see the treasures that are there for us all:

- Lord, the light of my life, shine out within my darkness.

- In the Lord I'll be ever thankful. In the Lord I will rejoice. Trust in God, do not be afraid. Our hearts are untroubled, the Lord is near.

- O Jesu Christe, in te confido [O Jesus Christ, I trust in you].

- In God alone my soul can find rest and peace. In God my peace and joy. Only in God my soul can find its rest, find its rest and peace.

All can be found in the English edition of *Sing to God*—a CD from the Taizé Community (© 1995 Ateliers et Presses de Taizé). The printed words are contained in many of the collections that have been published over the years.

Music has been very therapeutic to those in the hospital, waiting with anxiety for operations or the reports from medical tests and examinations. It would be very helpful if we made certain that our family or friends knew what music we would like on such occasions and how to obtain a portable player to be taken to our bedside. When it would be most useful, there is little time to sort out all the arrangements, so it is important for us to be prepared beforehand. We want to be able to recognize the music as our "favorite" at the point of crisis. "Good music" is good only when it is good for us in our time of need or enjoyment. Let's make the discovery for ourselves early so that we can draw on it in times of need.

## Scripture

Within the Bible are many passages that will bring peace and encouragement to us in times of crisis. We need to mark such passages when we come across them, or collect a set of references. Some organizations have made bookmarks on which some key texts are recorded for easy reference. The artistic among my readers might like to create such a treasure for themselves and perhaps make some for their friends. If you have a concordance, you could look up such words as "trust," "peace," "light," and "hope."

The Psalms are a great treasury of riches for us to use when we are faced with the storms of life. Obviously, the writers had a lot of experience of such storms in a variety of situations. Not all of them will fit exactly into our experience. I hope that not too many of us suffer loss through battles of war. However, if we can see the language as metaphorical, it will often parallel our situation, and we can find it helpful. We may not always want to use the whole of a psalm, but instead repeat key verses a few times to let them reach into our minds and then put the rest of the psalm to one side. Again, it is good to make a list of your favorite psalms and to leave it handy for your use. I have picked out four examples in one of the newer translations of the Psalter.[1] The translation that we use regularly is probably the most helpful for us because of the memory factor. On the other hand, some more recent translations or paraphrases of the words make them so vivid that they speak more directly to our crisis situations.

### Psalm 56: Be merciful to me O God, for my assailants are treading me down.

In this psalm, there is this key verse, 3:

> When I am afraid, O God Most High,
> I will put my trust in you.

### Psalm 121: I lift up my eyes to the hills.

The psalm has these words of faith in verse 8:

> The LORD shall take care
>     of your going out and your coming in, from this time forth and forever.

### Psalm 124: If the LORD had not been on our side…

Verse 7 of this psalm is one we could use in a crisis:

> Our help is in the name of the LORD,
> who has made heaven and earth.

---

[1] © The Anglican Church in Aotearoa, New Zealand, and Polynesia. Used with permission from *A New Zealand Prayer Book / He Karakia Mihinare o Aotearoa* (London: Collins, 1989).

**Psalm 23: The Lord is my shepherd.**
This psalm that so many people know by heart has this encouragement in verse 4:

> Though I walk through the valley of the shadow of death,
> I will fear no evil,
> for you are with me,
> your rod and your staff are my comfort.

The psalmists seem to mirror so many of the emotions that we have in a variety of situations that their writings have long been the medium for the prayers and longings of God's people. They reflect all the messages of hope and the cries of frustration. They express our pain and our pleas for help. They give voice to our shouts of praise and complaint. Above all, they allow us to be ourselves in the presence of God and to know that God will patiently hear all our cries and respond with love. That love may be comfort or it may be challenge, but it is always working for our good.

**Prayer**

What I have just written should be an encouragement to our pattern of prayer in times of crisis. God will hear us, whatever we have to say. God will understand that when we are hurt, we sometimes say hard things. In our prayers, it is important to leave space for God to make a reply. We must listen as well as speak if we are to gain encouragement and realism. We need both to face up to a crisis. In the hope that these words might inspire your own in the time of a storm, in the following text I have set out three different types of prayer. They are not written as samples to be used, as much as examples that might help you see what sort of sentiments are likely to arise in your soul in such situations.

> *Christ Jesus, when the storms of life overtake us,*
> *you call us to face them with courage and faith.*
> *As I turn to you again, speak your word of peace to my heart,*
> *and your word of stillness to my mind.*
> *Guide me through the darkness*
>     *and point me in the way I should go.*
> *O Spirit of God, uphold me,*
> *and give me the fellowship of friends to support me*
>     *with words and with prayers.*
> *Keep me from panic and grant me perseverance*
> *until I can see the future unfolding.*

*Then heal my wounds with love
and give me energy for my tasks.
Gracious God, hear the prayer I offer
    and let me hear your word to me.
My God, you listened to the psalmists of old
when they cried to you in the turmoil of loss and pain.
Hear me now as I cry before you with tears of bewilderment,
with shouts of anger and moans of emptiness.
I am shocked and numbed, and there seems no way of escape.
Why did you let it happen, O God,
when you promised protection to those who loved you?
Why, O why, O why?
Is there any hope? If there any future?
Can I trust in you, or anyone else, again?
Are you sleeping, O my God?
There are times I hate you and even life itself.*

**Pause**

*And yet when I cry and shout, I feel you listening to my words.
When the anger subsides, I lift my eyes from their tears
to see the flicker of the light of hope.
I know you understand, O my Jesus,
for your cross speaks more loudly
than any smooth words of comfort.
In your agony, you let God have it too
before you found the words of releasing faith.
Like you, my Lord, I commit my spirit into your trusty hands.
Carry me with compassion for a while
and let me rest gently in your arms.*

**Pause**

*Together in your spirit, we will arise
to find new hope and new life.
Your love alone is my protection and my shield.
Your resurrection is my hope. Your Spirit is my power.
Your way is my future. Your peace is my perseverance.
Your kingdom is my only way, now and forever.
Caring God, your peace calms my soul,
whenever I face the crises of life.
Rekindle my faith again, and revive my hope for the future.
I look to you for guidance in my present trouble
and know from the past that with your help
    I can see it through.*

*Grant me a clear mind and a peaceful heart.*
*Strengthen my resolve to put into practice*
*those hard decisions I know I have to make.*
*Let your Spirit go on working in my heart*
*to bring healing and harmony to us all.*
*For your love's sake. Amen.*

Let's finish this chapter with some poetic verses[2] to sum it all up.

When the storms of life are o 'er us,
When the wind blows hard behind,
When the clouds are dark and threatening,
Then the Christ-star we must find.

Let the leap of every dolphin,
Soon restore our sense of hope,
And our trust in God Eternal,
Keep us safe till we can cope.

In the stillness finding Jesus,
Through the Spirit, freeing pain,
With firm faith hold fast the anchor,
Till we travel on again.

Then we'll cast our nets with courage,
We will search until we find,
Giving glory to our Savior,
Fish and Bread to all mankind.

---

[2] © Peter Atkins 1998. These verses may also be sung as a hymn to the tune "Omni Die," 87.87.

# 7
# Intercession and Healing

## Intercession

In the previous chapter, I mentioned the support of the prayers of friends in a time of crisis. This is known as the work of intercession. We use this word for those prayers that are for others rather than ourselves. In such prayers, we ask for help and blessing, in all their various forms, for those known personally or generally to us. In ordinary use, an intercessor is one who takes the issues that face one person, or a group of people, and presents them to someone who can assist. In some parts of the world, we might call this person an advocate or a spokesperson. Through prayers of intercession, we speak on behalf of others to Almighty God. For example, we can address God on behalf of the poor who feel that they have no voice. Or we can pray to God on behalf of those fighting one another and who are so blinded by rage that they cannot see why they should seek the help of God to bring peace. We may also address God on behalf of the dying who are too ill to pray much for themselves. Bound together in the Christian community, it is right that we should speak to God in prayer for another part of the church in need at the time.

Yet to leave our understanding of intercessory prayer at that point would give a distorted picture of our theology of God. We dare not see God as unaware of what is happening in the world. Through our prayers we do not give information to a God who is ignorant of our condition or that of others, or of the events and situations that have occurred in our world. Neither does God need persuasion to do what is loving, right, and helpful for others. We do not intercede with a reluctant God who has to be reminded to do the right thing. The writer of the epistle to the Hebrews pictures Christ as already at prayer, interceding constantly for the world (Heb. 7:25).

Through our intercessions we become partners with the ascended Christ in creating the spiritual energy to provide guidance and strength to all those who need help. The task of intercession is to share with Christ in upholding the creation so that it has the power to reach the fulfillment of the purpose for which it was created. There is a wonderful window in the large worship space at the ecumenical community at Taizé in France. The window depicts the ascended Christ dressed in blue against the blue sky. In his hands he holds up the golden globe of the universe next to his heart. That window symbolizes what Christ does in prayer. He holds each one of us, and the whole universe, in place. We cannot slip out of his hands of love. Through his prayers, he keeps the circle of all things in their proper place so that we remain in touch with God and with one another. To be in that place of "connectedness" is to be whole. This idea is stated in the Hebrew language by the word *shalom*, which is otherwise translated as "peace." Peace only comes about when everything fits into its proper place. Peace is not the absence of tension, but the presence of all things in relation with all other things, including God. So there is peace and wholeness when everything relates properly to everything else. Our prayers of intercession are part (with Christ) of the work of holding everything in its proper place and applying our spiritual energies to help keep them in touch with God. When we intercede, we are often restoring the circle of touch for those who are disjointed and out of touch with God and with others. In electrical terms, we are like a circuit connector that, when in place, allows the energy to flow again into all parts of the circuit. Holding our hands together in prayer can be a useful symbol of this task. Then we are using a symbol to convey the meaning of the words:

Gracious God, let your divine power flow into the lives of_____, which will enable them to be reconciled and related to you and all those about them.

## Praying and Doing

Asking for divine strength is one part of our prayers for others. Asking for guidance to fulfill the will of God is another part of the prayer. "What should be done for them?" is a question not only for God but for us as partners with God in the coming of the kingdom of

God. Intercession demands not only spiritual energy from us but also clarity of thought and purpose. When we pray for the poor, we enter into their condition (indeed we may belong to "the poor"), and our prayers are part of the discernment about how the prayer should be answered. Divine grace and human endeavor work side by side in intercession. The earth must be blessed for us to have food to share, but human beings must weed out greed and selfishness for all to have what is sufficient for their basic needs. This is probably why in the Lord's Prayer the words "Give us today our daily bread" are followed by "and forgive us our sins." The problem for most of the world's poor is not that there are insufficient resources to go around, but that some people have far more than they need and others less than is necessary. Our prayers for the poor should also include prayers for the rich! The poor need help in reorganizing their lives to be able to move from poverty to self-sufficiency. The rich need help in knowing the joy of sharing so that at the feast in the kingdom of God the table has enough for the needs of all.

When we intercede for those at war with one another—within families, communities, and nations—we are adding our spiritual strength to the peacemakers who need sustaining in that role. With them, we will ask: "What should be done?" The establishment of peace will mean that justice will be done; hurts forgiven; violence restrained; differences respected; and each person seen as part of our common humanity, not of a rival group. To achieve this goal, people will have to be put in touch with others as potential friends and neighbors, not as strangers and enemies. Through our prayers and the grace of God, individuals will be empowered to act as peacemakers—and we may also be called to such a role.

Gathering information and sharing communication are part of the work of intercession. To pray well, our minds must be informed and our spirits attuned to God's revelation. When we pray we will communicate whenever possible with those who are the subject of our prayers. Modern means of communication make this so much easier and quicker with the telephone, the fax, and e-mail. It is important that we contact those for whom we pray to let them know of our concern, of our prayers, and of our faith that God will bless them with guidance and strength. We should also gather as much information as we can about every situation. Informed intercessors will be effective partners with God in offering assistance to those for whom they pray. The information is not simply to know the facts but to reflect on the question, What can be done about the situation?

When our intercessory prayers are effective, they usually result in some practical actions on behalf of those for whom we pray. In my own city, it is good to see so many congregations collecting food each week at the Sunday services to be made up into food parcels to give a helping hand to hungry families. This makes our prayers for the needy possible without hypocrisy. Prayer without action is shallow. Action without prayer is materialistic. The poor need more than food parcels. They too need the gifts of spiritual strength and guidance. Our societies also have structural problems that must be addressed if we are to lift people out of poverty. There are questions of employment and wages, of housing and health, of motivation and positive role models, of dependency and corporate responsibility. Our prayers of intercession may well lead us to join an action group dedicated to seeking God's guidance about what can be done in a situation. The combined wisdom and actions of Christians with powers of leadership and responsibility can be effective in working through some of the solutions to the contributory problems that have caused the situation that is the subject of our intercession. I note that the first Christians worked out practical ways of alleviating the poverty of some in their group and appointed members "full of faith" and prayer to attend to the details (Acts 6:1–6). As individual Christians at prayer, some of our soul time might be spent in identifying "soul mates" who might search with us to find an answer to the question "What can be done about the situation?" that we identified in our prayers.

## Healing

Much of the work of intercession seems to be focused on prayers for healing the sick. Up to this point, I have shared some thoughts about other subjects of intercession so that we can see the breadth of the topic. However, it is time now to share my understanding of prayers for healing. Then we can end the chapter with some practical hints and an example of a liturgy of intercession.

Prayers for healing highlight many of the issues about praying for others. Consider these:

1. How does God respond to our prayers?
2. What is the "will of God" for those who are sick?
3. What part does faith play in healing?
4. Whose faith is vital—the one who prays or the one prayed for?
5. Is full recovery from sickness the only positive response to prayers for healing?

6. How much of healing depends on prayer and intercession?
7. What is a miracle?

We have to face these kinds of questions if we are to be involved in intercession for the sick. We can, of course, avoid them by declaring that the work of healing belongs to God in Christ alone and that human agents have no part to play. Some people who think this way use the text: "The LORD gave, and the LORD has taken away, blessed be the name of the LORD" (Job 1:21). Such an attitude of resignation removes human responsibility and ignores the call of Christ to his disciples to be partners in prayer and work with God. In the numbness of shock and grief, it may be an inevitable attitude for the Christian to take, but it is not valid theologically in the longer term. The evidence is that human beings are responsible for caring for the body and for assisting its recovery through prayer and practical support. So it is right for us to face up to these questions.

Let's take them slowly, one at a time, and I suggest that you reread what I have written until you have shaped an answer that, with faith, you feel is right. If the answer still confuses you, then find a soul mate to share your thinking and pray together about it.

**How Does God Respond to Our Prayer?**

First, God responds with thankfulness and joy that we are sharing in the work of intercession on behalf of those who are sick. God's next response would be one of acknowledgment that God cares about the situation, is already aware of it, is working for its resolution, and is looking for human cooperation and partnership. In human language, God might say: "I welcome this prayer. I hear. I care. I act. I wait in hope."

**What Is the Will of God for Those Who Are Sick?**

There are two major principles in God's creation that we should keep in mind. They are the principles of recovery and mortality. Creation is designed both to recover from hurts and diseases and to have a limited life span. The gospel adds a further good news principle. God has a gift for those who desire it with faith—the gift of resurrection. This is a new existence that defeats death as the end of all life. This resurrection is a gift and not a "right." It is a new existence, not a part of the "old" created order. So the will of God must be to fulfill these principles for the sick—recovery, mortality, and the gift of resurrection. During most of the time span of our lives, our bodies are in recovery mode. We can live positively with the various limitations set by our bodies. In times of sickness, our bodies need special care, good space, ample time, and whatever medical help is available to facilitate such recovery. If our souls are in turmoil, it can seriously retard such recovery. In times of stress, our bodies are more open to the causes of sickness. We are more aware now than for many generations past how much soul-care keeps our bodies healthy, and how disease spreads in times of turmoil in an individual, a society, or a community. When we are sick, prayers of intercession support our own prayers for the "shalom" of our soul. This, in turn, gives our bodies the best circumstances for recovery from sickness to take place. Medicine and surgery will also support the body when administered with loving care and skill.

As we become aware of our bodies, we are also conscious of their limitations and mortality. Much has been done to alleviate those limitations; my glasses to restore sight are an example that comes to mind as I write. Wheelchairs, computers, and drugs are other examples in a wide and complex range. Yet we must acknowledge that, despite all these aids, our bodies are created for a limited existence on earth, and that is also part of the "will of God."

The gifts of God not only include recovery but also the courage and grace to live with limitations and mortality and the promise of resurrection when our span of mortal life is concluded.

## What Part Does Faith Play in Healing?

Faith (in the sense of trust in God and other people) is a vital ingredient in the process of recovery and in the reception of the gift of resurrection. If our souls are fighting those who are trying to help and support us, then our bodies may reject or delay the process of recovery. Faith is that quality that causes us to work positively toward recovery or acceptance. It relaxes the body and gives it "peace," that feeling of being in touch with God and with love. We no longer feel isolated because we are sick or because we think that we are rejected, are less than human, or are guilty of some great sin. Faith restores our will to live whatever the circumstances or gives us the will to accept the gift of resurrection. Within the context of ultimate meaning and purpose, faith in God is a priority. Within a more restricted view of our human context, faith in other human beings operates for our welfare. With faith, we will trust those who are working with us for recovery or acceptance. Without such trust, our healing is held back or our acceptance of God's gift is thwarted by fear or anger.

## Whose Faith Is Vital—The One Who Prays or the One Prayed For?

Faith is both personal and corporate. The famous quotation from the poet John Donne is true about faith as well as living: No one is an island. Our individual faith lives and grows in a sea of communal faith. When I am sick, I trust doctors and nurses, not only because of my own personal experience, but even more because the community sees them as trustworthy. My faith in God is always supported by the faith of those around me and by those who pray for me, whether that be my own family or my Christian community and friends. So the faith of the pray-er and the prayed-for intertwine and affect each other. In one biblical story of Jesus' work as a healer, the emphasis is on the faith of the friends of the sick man (Mk. 2:5). In another passage, the faith of the sick person is commended by Jesus and is said to contribute to the recovery (Mk. 5:34). What is important in our intercession is that we communicate our prayer and our faith not only to God but to the person whom we are supporting with our prayers. That sick person may first have faith in us and then discover a faith in God at a later stage. Obviously, if the sick person exercises his or her own faith in God and prays to God, then the situation will be even more positive. Remember, God's spirit inspires faith, so our prayers are effective at that point as well.

## Is Recovery from Sickness the Only Positive Response to Prayers for Healing?

The first expectation we should have when we pray for the sick is that they should recover so they can live well within the normal limitations of their bodies. We pray in this way because this is the usual experience of recovery. As our prayers of intercession for the sick are ongoing, they will always be offered in the light of the current circumstances as we know them. We have seen that a sick person's greatest need is for soul support. This leads to faith and the grace to allow the recovery process to take place.

Our prayers will also recognize that the body may only partially recover or that the mortal body may die. In the face of this possibility, our prayers will then be that the sick person can accept the appropriate gifts from God—grace to live positively with limitations or grace to accept the gift of resurrection.

Our prayers are always for the "wholeness" of the person. We are whole when we are able to live fully within the body that we have. It is never a perfect body, but it is nearly always a useful body. I am full of admiration for those who live a "whole" life with a very restricted body. They show us that wholeness is a matter of the soul rather than the body. Yet we need a body for this life, and we trust that God will provide us with the "body" for the life of resurrection.

## How Much of Healing Depends on Prayers of Intercession?

You have probably by now worked out an answer to this question for yourself from what I have written already. Check out your conclusions with these notes.

1. When we are sick, we need support. The prayers of others are part of that support and cooperate with Christ's prayer.
2. When we are sick, we need faith and trust. Prayers of intercession share and inspire such faith.
3. Our pattern of recovery or acceptance flows out of soul care. Prayers of intercession strengthen this care.
4. Recovery and resurrection are gifts from God. Our prayers encourage thankful acceptance of these gifts.
5. Healing occurs when we are in touch with our Creator, with our "neighbors," and with ourselves. Prayers of intercession help the sick to get in touch with all those around them.

In this sense, healing does depend on prayers of intercession, which is why they are part of every corporate service of the church. Our personal prayers are an essential part of that corporate activity.

## What Is a Miracle?

There is great confusion about the concept of miracles as they relate to prayers of intercession. A miracle seems to be defined as an extraordinary outcome that defies the normal expectation of recovery and proves that God is more powerful than medical science. As Christians we can define a miracle as the gift of God given and received through grace and prayer. God always offers us the appropriate gifts—wholeness for the soul, recovery or resurrection for the body. The miracle is that God always has our full welfare at heart. Recovery of the body is not a sign of greater love than the welfare of the soul or the gift of resurrection.

Any attempt to say that a "miracle" of the unexpected recovery of the body is dependent on the quality of faith—either of the sick person or the person interceding—denies that God is overwhelmingly generous. We have already clarified the place of faith in the answer to prayer. So in some ways all of God's gifts are "miracles"—a source of wonder to us and actions beyond anything that we deserve. We should give thanks to God for life itself—lived here or in eternity. Many of those who look for miracles are very limited in what they see as the parameters of life and, for them, only one outcome is worth having. In such circumstances, they may attempt to bargain with God—and we may do so too until we can reach the point of acceptance of the gift of resurrection just as readily as the gift of recovery.

As you pause in reading this chapter, you might like to offer this prayer of intercession for those who are sick:

*Creator God, you made us and all creation.*
*You give us the gifts of recovery and resurrection.*
*We join our prayer to the prayer of Christ for all those who are*
    *sick, especially* _____
*Give them grace, strength, and courage*
    *as they wait with patience for the recovery of the body [for the*
    *gift of resurrected life].*
*Give them an assurance of your love and our love for them;*
*enable those who support them with medical care, with skill, and*
    *tenderness;*
*increase in us all faith in your goodness*
    *and gratitude for your gifts of life,*
*for this world and for eternity.*
*We offer this prayer for your love's sake.*
*Amen.*

## Practical Guidance for Intercessory Prayer

We must take steps to see that intercessory prayer does not become a burden to wear us out rather than a joy to fulfill in our soul time. To prevent being weighed down by this type of prayer, let me remind you of some points of theology and share with you some practical hints.

Our theology of intercessory prayer is that it is a corporate activity with the ascended Christ and with the whole church, the total Christian community. We are part of the team of intercessors, so the task does not fall totally on us. To play our part, we need to have faith in God, deep love for others, an ability to offer and sustain prayer, and a willingness to be organized. We also need to be informed, discerning, and ready to add practical action to our prayers.

The methods used to offer intercessory prayer vary to suit our different personality preferences. Some like to use prayers taken from a prayer book, while others prefer to use their own words for these prayers. Some people like to use "arrow" prayers scattered throughout the day. They create quick spaces for prayer and "hold" a situation or person in the presence of the praying Christ for God's blessing to flow upon it or them. Others like to create a defined space in a day when they can pray for others as well as themselves. Early morning, noon, and the end of the day are traditional times for these prayers to be made. However, an individual can set aside any time to fit in with her or his program.

Within the time and space available, focus your mind on the praying Christ. Realize that you will be pouring out your spiritual energy in this time of prayer. Let your mind be focused on the people for whom you are praying. Let your heart pour out love and strength. Clarify what you see as the desired outcome. Reflect on what actions can be taken to assist the situation.

Your prayers should include people who are known to you personally and those people and situations more generally known. Christ calls us to share in the total work of intercession, so we cannot limit ourselves to the narrow focus of those people and situations that touch us closely. It has to be a "both/and" activity. We will pray for good government as well as good health for our friends, for peace and justice in nations as well as in our family circle. On the other hand, we will avoid "doing a global"—that is, covering the world's needs in a few phrases. We will also be thoughtful enough not to allow our prayers to degenerate into a "shopping list" of requests to God—composing a "God please help this and that" list of twenty items!

We will therefore need a structure for our work of intercessory prayer. Here again, we need flexibility to suit our circumstances. One possibility is to take a theme for each day of the week. Another is to cover a wider range by allocating a theme or geographical area of the world to each day of the month. There is no "correct" method—only one that makes your prayers effective and fulfilling, knowing that Christ and the church are alongside you in a team situation.

Here is an example of a plan for such prayers based on a theme for each day of the week.

*Monday:* The workplace; those waiting for employment; justice in the economic system; those facing the tensions and crises of work decisions.

*Tuesday:* Reconciliation and peace; the leaders and people of those nations in the midst of conflict; refugees; adults and children in places of violence; agencies for peace.

*Wednesday:* Learning and wisdom; our schools, universities, and training institutes; those doing research; those defining ethical positions; our own children and godchildren.

*Thursday:* Community responsibility; those in government, locally, nationally, and globally; the police and social service agencies; those in prison and before the courts; our selected charity; our immediate family and extended family.

*Friday:* The suffering and the carers; those who are sick or limited in body; all who support and care for them; the medical scientists and hospital administrators; the dying and the deserted; those in grief and loss.

*Saturday:* The Sabbath; people of other faiths; those entering into marriage; those involved with entertainment and leisure; shopkeepers; the overworked.

*Sunday:* The Christian community worldwide; your local Christian community; those coming to faith; the resurrected community of heaven; Christians in persecution.

Within such a framework, try to make your prayers of intercession as specific as possible, but do not go into endless detail. Remember again that God knows and cares and does not need to be persuaded to do what is best for the person or situation.

Some people are helped to feel that their prayers are effective by writing down the subject of those prayers and leaving the paper before the symbol of the cross or icon in their soul space. Others want to speak the prayer out loud. Still others form a picture of the person or situation in their minds and imagine God's stretching forth a hand in blessing on them. Decide what the best method is for your and then use it without embarrassment.

On occasion in your soul time, you may want to use a more structured form of intercession. This may be when you are tired and want assistance or when you feel you need a change of pattern. I conclude this chapter with an example. It suggests the use of candles, incense, and various symbols, though of course these are not essential. As I am suggesting a change of style, some will find them helpful. This liturgy could also be used when, in your time of intercession, you are joined by one or two other people. Each one could then take responsibility for a section in turn.

## A Liturgy of Intercession

**A Christ candle is lit.**
Gracious God, always ready to give us what we need,
we thank you for your many gifts to us and to all your creation.
We join with Christ as we uphold in prayer
> those who are dear to your heart and ours:
> those with great responsibility for decisions
> in your world and ours;
> those at turning points in their lives;
> and those in the midst of suffering and heartache.

As we pray for others in this time of intercession,
we pause to draw strength
from your Holy Spirit to enable our prayers
> and empower our actions.

**A smaller candle (one for each intercessor) is lit and silence kept for a time.**
First, I uphold in prayer my family_____; my friends_____;
> and my neighbors_____.

Give them your guidance and protection.
Strengthen their faith and love,
and restrain them from evil.
Uphold them in love as they_____.
Give them talents for their work and joy in the delights of life.
Help me to know my part in making
> the best possible things happen for them.

God of love, grant them your blessing of love.

**A stick of incense may be lit and allowed to burn.**
Lord of Creation,
you are powerful in your care
> and responsibility for the universe.

I uphold before you in prayer those who are entrusted
with the power of decision making on behalf of us all:
> those in government and
> members of representative assemblies;
> those who decide policy and
> carry it out for the public good;
> those who are leaders in industry and commerce;
> those in the world assemblies
> who seek to maintain peace, reconciliation, and justice;
> those whose voices are raised to protect the environment;

*Intercession and Healing* 103

    those who suffer from the decisions of the powerful and
        are crushed by greed and exploitation.
Especially I pray today for_____.
Guide them in righteousness, strengthen them in purpose;
    restrain the overpowering, raise up the meek,
    and cause them all to seek your will.
God of power, grant them your guidance.

**A symbol of the cross is placed on an article or picture from a newspaper or magazine depicting suffering.**

God of compassion, your love reaches out both to those who
    suffer and to those who cause such suffering.
Sustain those who suffer, ease their affliction,
    hear their cries of pain.
Restrain the sinners, strike their consciences,
    hold back their violence and their greed,
    bring them to repentance and forgiveness.
Through the cross of Christ, journey with the smitten,
    restore their sense of dignity,
    and rouse the compassion of us all
    to help them rebuild their lives.
Especially I pray for_____.
God of the cross and resurrection, grant them your hope.

**A flower may be placed next to the Christ candle.**

God of beauty, with you we pray for the restoration of all that
    is damaged and disfigured.
    We uphold in prayer:
    all who have who been abused or misused;
    all who live in concrete jungles where the bully reigns;
    all who are tortured for their faith or conscience;
    all marred by accidents;
    all who are told they are worthless;
    all dependent on drugs or alcohol.
Especially I pray for_____.
Let your beauty touch their lives again,
    and restore their sense of worth as lovely in your eyes.
Create in them a picture of the future
    as it can be in your good purpose.
God of recovery, grant them your re-formation.

**The hands of the intercessor may be lifted up.**

Gracious God, hear these our prayers and give to us and all
    your people sensitivity of mind, warmth of heart,

>     and strength of arm,
>     to work for what we have prayed for,
>     even the doing of your will.
> Abba God, grant us all your peace.
> In Christ's name we pray. Amen.

## Summary

Intercessory prayer is part of the activity of the kingdom of God. It is our joyful responsibility to pray and work to bring the will and plan of God to fruition. We join with Christ and the whole Christian community in supporting others and in seeking God's blessing for all people and for the whole of creation. We have learned some practical ways to make our prayers more effective.

# 8
# Cultural and Gendered Views of God

Each of you reading this book belongs to a gender, an age, and a culture, and these are likely to be very different from my own. As I have been using words like *God, us, people, Jesus, others*, you have been interpreting their meaning within your own experience and context. In this chapter it is time to explore what effects our pictures of God and people have on our common understanding of the words that we use to convey faith, truth, and experience.

## Your Picture of God

When we use the word *God* at the beginning of a prayer, what picture comes into your mind? If you are good at drawing or painting, take time at this point to depict the image(s) on paper. If you are a word-artist, write a poem or a paragraph under the title "God, I see you as…" If you find it best to put your ideas into the form of a prayer, start a prayer of thanksgiving with the words "God, I give you thanks that you are…"

Do try and complete the task I have just outlined before you read on! You need your own images before the rest of the chapter will make good sense and touch your prayer life in a meaningful way.

Look at your picture, word-picture, or prayer and ask yourself: How has that picture taken shape? What experiences, models, teaching, and visions have contributed to my current understanding of God? To help you with the answers to those questions let me give you some sources.

## Through Teaching

This is likely to be from our early experiences in the home, when we attended school, during the youth activities of our church or community, when we read the Bible or some parts of it, or religious books, when we listened to sermons in church, when we read magazines, or while we were members of a study group. In a whole variety of ways, we have been taught that God is like this or that, and sometimes this and that do not fit easily together. Some of these images were conveyed to us in nouns—love, light, justice, truth. Some of these images were given in the form of adjectives—powerful, merciful, good, righteous, holy. Some of these images are shaped by being likened to someone—father, shepherd, healer, king, guide.

Some of the teaching from the Bible comes in the form of stories. God is included in the stories of the garden of Eden, of Isaiah's experience of worship in the temple in Jerusalem, Jacob's wrestling in the desert, Elijah and the still small voice at the entrance to the cave in a storm, of the calling of Samuel in the night in the tabernacle of God at Shiloh. In the New Testament there is the record of the stories (also called parables) that Jesus told about God as a father to a prodigal son, or as a man awakened by the persistent visitor in the night. The New Testament also pictures God as the hearer of Jesus' prayers in the garden of Gethsemane and on the cross.

The material that we have been taught has influenced our thinking, though most Christians have absorbed it without critical examination and certainly without much open debate. Such teaching tended to be delivered on the principle that "I am telling you the truth" rather than "I am sharing with you what might be helpful for you in putting together a meaningful picture of God." However you were taught, take a moment now to identify those people who taught you helpfully and give thanks to God for their gifts to your faith.

> *God of great variety, I thank you for all those who shared with me*
> *the truth about you as they saw it, especially for _____.*
> *Thank you, God, for their gifts and their faith,*
> *for their trust in you, and their willingness to look for you*
> *and to be found by you.*
> *Help me to treasure the gifts they shared with me,*
> *and to see how they can form a part of my current*
> *understanding of you,*
> *the one I worship and live for.*
> *Open my mind to know you and my heart to love you.*

*In the power of the Spirit and in the name of Christ, I make this prayer. Amen.*

**Through Experience**

As we discovered in the first chapter of this book, all of us have some deep personal experiences of God, which have all contributed to our current picture of the Godhead. Such experiences come from visions, voices, pictures, and holy spaces. These experiences have given us ideas of holiness, communication, relationship, awe, and maybe even love, worth, generosity, and goodness. Some of these experiences, we found, were with a "power" and some with a "person." Recall again now some of the most important for you.

**Through Models**

Most of what we have been taught has not left a distinct pattern in our minds, but has created a fabric of current knowledge, whose threads are only seen if brightly colored. On the other hand, our teachers have been powerful models. If the teacher modeled what was being taught, then a much greater impression was left on our souls. If someone taught us about forgiveness and was a good model of how to forgive, then we will have a much better understanding of forgiveness. If we were taught about a God of love in our home, then the models of loving behavior that we saw will be very powerful in establishing what God's love might be like. We will not be restricted to the actual examples because our minds are capable of grasping the concept of love. This is constructed from a variety of examples, longings, and teachings. However, it is true that the actual models that translate a concept into reality are a vital part of teaching.

We also build up our pictures of God from models in the form of art. Pictures that hang in the home, the school, the church, and the museum leave a lasting impression on our minds. They help us shape our thoughts and ideas. They give our minds something tangible on which to hang our ideas. For those who have attended a church, stained-glass windows and statues can be powerful symbols of God that we have seen and perhaps touched. Part of the mind is well aware that the objects are only a concept of the reality as conveyed to us by the artist. In another part of our minds the association of feelings and experiences is so powerful that the window or the statue can become the channel of our relationship with the reality itself. The attitude of different parts of the Christian community to these "models" varies. I believe that this variation is in accordance with the basic nature of the different personalities. Some who see a symbol use it as a springboard for associated ideas. Others have a mind that fixes on the symbol itself and its limitations. Both attitudes are valid in their own right. Mutual respect and learning are important so that one group does not disrespect or restrain the other because they do not see things in the same light. It will be a sad day when we worship the idol and not the Creator God. Yet it will be a sad day when we lose color and symbol from our worship in some attempt to be purely spiritual. In such a process the principle of the incarnation can be lost.

That leads me to refer to the most powerful model of the Godhead for most Christians—*the model of Jesus Christ.* Christians see Jesus as being the model of the God about whom he taught his disciples, and of the religious truths and behaviors that God upholds. The epistle to the Colossians declares Jesus to be in "the image of the invisible God" (Col. 1:15). Jesus' teaching and life are all at one with God's will, nature, and being. For many Christians, Jesus is the effective "symbol" of the Godhead, and his person is the one to whom we can relate. Many like to have a picture of Jesus in their minds when they pray. Their teaching about God tells them that the nature of the Godhead is larger than the incarnate figure of Jesus Christ. However, their souls find it easier to gaze upon the representation of God in the face of Jesus Christ.

The use of models, pictures, and statues may have limitations. The language of our prayers may restrict us as well. The use of the word *Father* as an address to God in prayer (taken from the English translation of *Abba* in Hebrew) tends to shape the gender of God. This was reinforced by the use of male nouns like king, shepherd, and judge when those roles were seen as exercised only by males. In English the use of the pronouns *he* and *his* to refer to God also confirmed a male image for God. In some of the parables that Jesus told, a male figure represents God (the father with two sons, the judge, the owner of the vineyard, and the shepherd are examples that come to mind). On the other hand, some other parables have a female figure that represents God (the woman who lost the coins, the woman who baked the bread with yeast, the hen with her brood of chickens). For many years no one seemed to point the latter out to a male-dominated church. In our minds we were aware that theological teaching always indicated that God was neither male nor female, but the models of God held up for us to see were almost entirely male. This was reinforced for many Western Christians by the way they so closely identified Jesus with God in their minds. There was (and is) no doubt that Jesus was male, and therefore people tended to think of God as male also. It is quite a shock to some people to suggest that this is too restricted a view to hold. It may be so for you as well, but I advise patience at this point. No one is asking you to throw away your picture of God. What you are asked to do is to allow a wider concept to be placed alongside it and to enlarge it.

## Cultural Images

Your picture of God has also been composed of cultural images. We tend to picture or describe God as "one of us." God wears the features of our face, our clothes, even our style of hair. Even if we do not see God as a person, the picture is likely to have our familiar colors, geography, and vegetation. Some symbols may be more universal throughout creation, but they will still be portrayed from our cultural perspective. If we use words to describe God, they will come from our familiar language with all the cultural associations that that language conveys.

For some of you, the above may be only marginally true. The way that we have conceived the Christian message may mean that the images of God come in an imposed cultural form. Christianity may not yet have become fully incarnated in your culture. One of the causes of this may have been the pictures illustrating the Bible when it was first in your hands and another the leadership of the missionary church who brought the gospel to your area. The problem with some Bibles printed in the last two centuries is that they often contained pictures set in a particular culture. The figure in the story of the good shepherd might be dressed in long flowing robes with the head covered in a head scarf. Jesus on the cross might be shown as an almost naked, tall, white, central European figure. The picture of Jesus blessing the children might bear no resemblance to any person of our race and culture. For this reason Jesus and God may not relate to our culture and generation, but perhaps be a stranger in our midst. In the field of art, many prime examples by world-renowned painters depict Jesus and the disciples as Italians of their particular generation against a background of the Tuscan hills and towns. Some of the painters' models for God were old men from their local villages. The culture was right for their people, but it does not fit with us. Even more powerful influences for some younger people have been the religious epic films coming out of Hollywood. Such films have fixed images in our minds. We see God as the actor in *The Ten Commandments.* Even though this is an age that values historical accuracy, there have been few attempts to show Jesus in films and art as a Hebrew by race, with features belonging to the people of the district of Nazareth at what we would call the beginning of the Christian era. Obviously, the intelligent Christian knows that Jesus came from Galilee, spoke the local language, and looked like one of the twelve disciples. Yet from the time of the ascension, the Christian community saw Jesus as identified with all of humanity, of whatever gender or culture or race or age. Jesus had shared fully in the basic conditions of being human, but not in the condition of every race, the other gender, and the more aged. This "limitation" of the incarnation to a particular place and people and time stresses the importance of that part of being human that is common to all. In this sense it is right to see Jesus as one of us without denying that he therefore must be at one with others who differ from us. The ascended Christ is not a stranger to us as a human being, but cannot ever be totally like the unique person we are. As this is true, we can give thanks that our picture of God can lie side by side with the picture that means most to our neighbors, even though those pictures will be different in many cultural aspects. We can move to a further stage and realize that the other pictures begin to broaden our own concepts of God. They will fill out a whole that is more than the sum total of the parts. There are things contained in my neighbor's picture that help me to see God from a new angle or give sharper focus to something that was blurred in my own picture.

## Exploring Other Images

I am suggesting that we retain our picture of God but also learn to transcend it and maybe even amend it from time to time. Discipleship is concerned with growth as well as faithfulness. For growth to occur, we must take the risk of leaving the familiar behind for a time in order to explore what new things come our way. So let's do some of this exploring.

Could our picture of God include some of the features of being female and of being male? For example, it might be helpful to address God in prayer in some of these ways:

"God, the Mother and Father of us all"
"God, our parent"
"God, you shelter us under your wings like a mother hen"
"God, our king and our queen"
"Ascended Christ, our sister and our brother"
"Jesus, sharer of our full humanity"
"Holy Spirit, giving birth to a new creation"

## Cultural and Gendered Views of God   111

The advantage of these more inclusive ways of addressing God would be that we can unconsciously draw on both male and female figures as models of the attributes of God. It would also mean that those of either gender could feel that they could fully relate to God "as one of us" without, of course, limiting God to being male or female. To address God in such terms will probably help us to be more aware that we are using these images as springboards for our communication with God, who transcends (but does not deny the validity of) being female and male. Maybe such inclusive language will help people handle their sexuality more adequately in their relationship with God. There is a lot of proper emotion in this relationship but, as with making friends with those of either gender, our emotions do not have to be suppressed just because they are not expressed sexually. Our feelings of love for God and others can be expressed emotionally without becoming sexual. When we reach this maturity, the "gender" in which we address God, whether it is male or female or inclusive of both, does not threaten to undermine the relationship and can in fact enlarge it.

Now we can explore the question of race and culture in our picture of God. Here people seem to prefer the more inclusive forms of address to God. They are comfortable with beginning their prayers with:

"God of every race"
"God of humanity"
"God of all the peoples of the world"

The form of the address is in their own languages, but they are also happy to include traditional Hebrew or Aramaic words such as *amen*, *hallelujah*, and sometimes *maranatha*. Within the Christian community we seldom restrict God as being only of our own race. It is true that to those of another race attending our worship we sometimes give the impression that God will be on our side and against another race in any conflict. The history of this century just concluding is sadly full of examples when races claimed God as fighting for their side in a conflict with neighbors. From the First Testament we sometimes get the idea that God is not only "one of us," but is also "for us" and "against them." As far as culture and language are concerned, we are sure God speaks "our" language, and we give the impression that God does not appreciate prayers unless they are in the "right" language, which of course is the one we like to use. The cultural ways of others in worship may be suppressed by our insistence on the proper form of the liturgy and the prayers.

Yet since the Christian community is made up of many different races and languages, deep down we know that it is right to pray to God as the one who relates to all races and hears each person in her or his own language and culture. I find it exciting to see God represented in a variety of cultural forms. When I was in Soweto in South Africa, it was good to see God depicted as a black African. I even saw a cross on which the figure of Christ was carved showing the features of a tribal leader of one of the tribes through the distinctive dress and pattern of teeth-carving. Some people of other races find this symbol difficult because it seems unrepresentative, forgetting the many pictures and windows in their culture in which Christ is shown as someone of their race.

## The Clash of Cultures

Some people experience another difficulty that arises from the predominant use of the word "Lord" attached to God or Jesus at the beginning of prayers. This word speaks of a cultural system of dominance. For some "Lord" is a "leftover" of medieval society, where the classes were divided into lords and servants. The lords gave the commands, and the servants humbly obeyed. Using these words and the concepts they contain gives a picture of God as the "all-powerful boss" and relegates us to the position of humble and obedient servants, with no part to play in the enterprise that is the subject of our prayers. You can see how this concept and language is in conflict with the ideas we have explored in this book. We have envisioned a God who calls us into partnership and friendship. It is for this reason that so many people want to call Jesus their friend rather than master. For others Jesus must be acknowledged as Lord to indicate that we are called to give our total commitment and loyalty to Christ and to clarify the proper roles in the divine-human relationship. It is God who takes the initiative, and as humans we respond to the divine, loving will with affection and adoration.

This dialogue illustrates well the clash of cultures that we often find in common prayer. The forms of address to God that some people find helpful because of their strong associations with religious experience are sometimes a cause of difficulty for others. Even the word "Father" has deep difficulties for some people because of their treatment at the hands of a human father. My suggestion is that we should never become dependent on just one form of address to God, such as "Almighty God" or "Heavenly Father" or "Lord" or "Father." In this book I have tried, in the written prayers, to model a wide range of ways to address God and to search for the one that is most appropriate for the content of the prayer.

All these possible difficulties about gender, race, and culture make some people want to picture God only in nonhuman terms. Their pictures are of light, rainbows, and radiant colors. This is where the attraction of New Age thinking comes in. In word pictures they will use truth, love, peace, wisdom, justice, mercy, joy, and wonder to describe God. Their relationship with God is with a "power" rather than with a "person," with mystery and not with material symbols, with a transcendent God who is beyond human understanding. Obviously, scripture and the theologians in many ages have given support to this more philosophical approach to God. It can avoid some of the confusion to be found in using human language for God. The hymn "Immortal, Invisible, God Only Wise" is a favorite hymn to express such thoughts.

However, to remove the *personal* nature from our understanding of God leaves out the heart of the relationship for which the soul yearns so strongly. Even when we want words that transcend the gender of God, we do not want to use "it" for God. We must not reduce God to a "thing," or we will take away the compassion and empathy of God for our human condition. We may also imagine we are under the control of a "force" with whom we cannot dialogue or to whom we cannot relate. As a follow-through to this idea of God as an invisible force, some young people speak of the "force that will get you." We fear what we do not know and cannot name. Without a relationship there can be no love, and love was at the heart of Jesus' message in the gospels. To speak of God as "only wise" could reduce the intercessor to asking merely for a revelation of such wisdom and not for insight to find, as a partner with God, the best solution for the situation. Humanity then becomes totally dependent on the directions that God gives and is incapable of playing a part in the discovery of the truth.

Some language used in prayer reduces God to a power that carries out functions. To speak of God only as Creator, Jesus as Redeemer, and the Spirit as Lifegiver focuses on the activity of God, but not on the heart of God. It would be the same as addressing a parent as the housecleaner, the office worker as typist, or the church leader as pastor. In the end, parents want to be remembered and spoken to as people—persons of value, not functionaries of usefulness. Our society is already tempted to depersonalize everybody. Our banker is reduced from John or Mary, who asks how we are as well as how much we want to withdraw, to an Automatic Teller Machine (ATM). In the supermarket the personal service is reduced to a checkout operator with a scanning machine. When I want to talk to someone on the telephone, I am directed to voice mail. Soon all of us will be able to do our shopping on the Internet, our personal mail will be delivered by fax instead of by a friendly person, and, of course, we may be tempted to enter into our worship by using the service on the television. People are becoming merely the adjunct of the machine. We started out with the reverse philosophy! In school the learning may be from a computer modem, not a teacher model. In such a world we can easily reduce people to objects of our pleasure and will rather than seeing them as people with feelings and personality, hopes and fears, longing for recognition and love. A very strong incentive to see human beings as people rather than things lies in the acknowledgment of God as having the attributes of personality as well as power and presence—that is the "I AM" of the scriptures. If humans are created in the image of God, then one of the basic conditions of being human is to relate personally both to God and to one another.

## God as Holy Spirit

So far I have said little about our picture of God as Holy Spirit. This is the central experience of God for many people in this age. In the 1960s attempts were made to reduce God to a mere possibility, and of little importance for humanity that had now come "of age." Even if it was admitted that there was a God, such a God was no longer relevant. Grown-up humanity did not need propping up. Humanity was strong enough to tackle the problems confronting it. Science would be the new savior of the world. Education would make people good. Machines would take away hardship and drudgery. Doubts were also expressed about the divinity of Jesus, and the focus among many Christian thinkers was on Jesus' example as a good human being whom we should emulate. The reaction to such reductionism was a new experience of God in a dramatic and immediate way. Signs and wonders were produced as a certain witness that God was not dead. Such wonders were to be found in spiritual healing and speaking in tongues. The new symbol for Christians was a dove rather than a cross. You may have included a dove in your picture of God, or the words Spirit or Holy Spirit in your word-picture or prayer. The association of the experience of the Holy Spirit is with feelings: touch, warmth of heart, otherness. The Spirit fills the believer with power and strength. The Spirit gives energy for the new life of righteousness and love. The Spirit rests on the head with the gentle touch of peace.

The emphasis on the experience of each individual makes it beyond challenge from any critical test. We can always reply to the doubter: "If I have experienced the Spirit's gift, you cannot tell me that it is not real for me because it is my experience." Some people did try to find external proof tests such as tithing, speaking in tongues, purity, and godly living. These could become hard, oppressive rules to test an inner experience that came in a variety of forms and in many different circumstances. The religion of the "spirit-filled" built up for itself a type of culture—praying in a certain form, raising hands in praise, falling over under the influence of the Spirit, singing choruses with repetition and emotion.

This may be *our* experience of God, and we know no other. The opposite may be true. You may be bewildered by what you have read in the previous paragraph, and, as something that is strange for you, you may condemn it. Be patient with difference and remember that we are exploring different cultural and gender views in this chapter. The object of our work in this soul time is to discover more about God and our relationship with God—and there is always more about God to discover.

## Checking Out the Pictures

As with other parts of the discovery path that we have traversed so far, it is important to examine them closely and not to think that we have to accept an "anything goes" type of principle in our understanding of God. To picture God entirely through the third Person of the Trinity—the Holy Spirit—is to leave out some of the essential truths about God. In the New Testament and in Christian theology, the Spirit is always associated with Jesus Christ and with God as the "I AM" of creation and salvation. We must not depersonalize the Spirit. The Holy Spirit is the spirit of the risen and ascended Christ. The Spirit's life-changing power creates in human beings the ability to live in accordance with the teachings and model of Jesus Christ. The life of love as lived by Jesus shared pain and suffering as well as victory over death. It cared for the outcast, forgave the sinner, affirmed the meek, and upheld the principles of righteousness and faith. Jesus also showed how people of both genders were equally important and that neither was dominant over the other. At Pentecost the Holy Spirit filled all those who responded in faith—both women and men, from every race and position in society. The experience of the Spirit touched not only the heart but the mind; it created community, not individualism. Our experience of the Spirit should be equally inclusive. The Spirit gave boldness to Christians, but it did not make them arrogant toward difference. They were to be humble as well as strong, gentle as well as burning with fire. These should be the marks of our experience and how we live in response to the revelation and gift of God the Holy Spirit.

How then can we fit our picture of God alongside that of others without reaching a point where there is nothing to hold in common? I advise you to identify those things in your experience of God that are currently important for you and then to see where you can find "growing edges." These are places where you can see that things can and should be changed, and where you recognize the challenge of God to develop a wider picture. You may wish to discard some images of God that are restrictive—such as, God is like an old man in the heavens sitting on a cloud, or God can only be portrayed in a cultural form like mine. You will be careful to include a wider pattern of address to God in your prayers and stop using Lord God or Father as the *only* forms. You will be open to those who have another way of experiencing God and will identify where you see the truth of what they say or do. Above all, you will stretch your mind and emotions to embrace the understanding of God "in Trinity." This incorporates a unity within the relationship of the Godhead, where God as parent and creator, Christ as son and redeemer, Spirit as personal presence and lifegiver, dwell together in perfect shalom and love. Our experience of God can never be great enough to grasp God's fullness, and God is never too great to be beyond our smallest attempts to reach out in prayer and faith.

After reflecting on what I have written and looking again at your picture of God in art or word, you might like to conclude with this prayer:

*God, touching the heavens and the earth,*
*and holding the smallest creature in your presence,*
*we draw near to your love in faith.*
*Help us to know you more fully,*
*to share our knowledge with our neighbor,*
*and to worship you in the community of the saints.*
*From the security of my culture, let me reach out to understand*
*how you embrace every culture*
*and delight in the variety of human beings.*
*From the security of my own gender,*
*let me reach out to understand*
*how you embrace both genders of humanity equally and delight in*
*our sexuality.*

*From the security of my own generation,
let me reach out to understand
how you embrace those of every generation,
from the newborn babe to the frail and old.
Then, in faith, will I find more of you, O God, revealed to me,
your own child, growing to maturity as your friend and partner,
ever loved and ever loving.
In the Spirit of love and in the name of Jesus Christ, I pray. Amen.*

# 9

# Sin and Forgiveness

In chapter 5, I promised to look at the question of sin and forgiveness in greater depth. In this chapter we can do that because we have built a firm relationship with God. Every relationship is created out of love. If the relationship is to endure, then that love must include the ability to embrace those who have hurt the relationship with words and actions. Such love must be strong enough to trust the other's positive response to a request for forgiveness. It is because we know that someone loves us that we feel secure enough to admit that we have done something that has hurt the relationship. That action may be the failure to see another's need, to give thanks for an act of generosity, to carry out an action of care, or to prevent a catastrophe. These are all acts of omission. On the other hand, the action that causes the damage to the relationship might be spiteful or arrogant words, violent behavior, deceit, or betrayal of trust. Those are all acts of commission; so we say that we have "committed" a sin when we do such things.

**Being Aware of Sinning**

How are we aware that we have done wrong? First, our conscience may tell us so. We are aware deep inside us that we have failed to do what we know was the "right" thing. We know that we are acting against the principles that we have set for ourselves. Such awareness leads to guilt and fear of the consequences. We are frightened that we will not be able to live with our conscience, that we are failures, and that we will not be strong enough to rebuild our principles. Second, we may realize that we have done wrong because we see the hurt that our actions have caused to others. The pain they show stings us into seeing the sin and the damage it has caused. Third, someone else may point out to us that what we have done or not done is a sin. At the time we sinned, we may have been unaware that we did anything wrong, but once it was pointed out to us with the reasons why it was wrong, we may be able to admit to ourselves that it was a sin. Fourth, the teaching of God in the scriptures and the church may convict us of sin. That means we measure our actions against the teaching and see that what we did was sinful.

God is at work in all these ways to stop us from continuing to sin. This is done for our sake as well as for the sake of the others who are hurt. We are aware that sin hurts everyone who is affected by it—and that includes the sinner. Sin leads to isolation, to the breakdown of relationships, to feelings of failure, or to deception about sin. In these ways sin is hurtful to the sinner. Sin also causes pain to others affected by the sin. Pain is important in our physical bodies; it is the warning bell that something is wrong. Pain is also positive in spiritual terms. It alerts us to the damage that we are causing to others as well as to ourselves. Pain tells the sinner and the sinned-against that sin is dangerous and should be stopped. Sin is also painful to God. It begins to destroy the relationship that has been built up between the person and God, and the person and his or her neighbors. The pain we see on the cross of Calvary is the ongoing reminder to us all of what happens when people sin. The cross shows us that we cannot say: "It does not matter what I do," or "No one was hurt by what I did," or "Sin has no consequences." When we look at the cross we can painfully see what sin does to people—and to God.

## Adam and Eve in the Garden

Turn to the story of the garden of Eden in the book of Genesis (say from chapter 2, verse 15 to the end of chapter 3), and read it again. Remember that this story is about the way Everyman (Adam) and Everywoman (Eve) acts when he or she sins. This story helps us reach a clear definition of sin and guilt.

The story illustrates that the root cause of sin is a refusal to admit that there are rules for living in God's creation. Sin arises out of the attitude that I can do anything I like, that I make up the rules, and that no one has a right to tell me what to do. It sounds very "modern," doesn't it? Every man and every woman, despite all the latitude and freedom, wants to be the final arbitrator of good and evil. They want to be gods—to take the place of the Creator. There are many frightening examples in history of those who thought that they alone made the rules—recall the names of a few emperors and a few modern dictators as "big" examples and a lot of other folk, on a smaller scale. They thought they could write a new set of regulations for living and left a stream of killed, maimed, and tortured people as their legacy.

Fortunately, in the story, Adam and Eve find out that they are naked. To know you are naked is to acknowledge your humanity and your mortality. You will remember that in a well-known fable the emperor loses his clothes and comes to realize that he is just another human being after all. At a time of death we say that we came into the world with nothing (we are naked), and we leave the world with nothing. When Adam and Eve realize that they are naked, they know that they are human and not gods, that they have done wrong to test the boundaries set by God. In doing so, they have broken the bond of the relationship and cannot face God. They hide in the garden. We all want to hide when our consciences convict us of sin. We try to do a "cover-up" job. We may want to move to a new space, bury ourselves in our own company, or become frantically busy to avoid thinking about the sin. We can even try to hide in the blur of a bottle of strong drink.

Yet for our own good and the good of the world, God will not let us hide for long. God takes the initiative and calls out to us. God does not accuse us by asking, "What have you done?" Instead God asks, "Why are you hiding in our relationship?" Here is the invitation to tell the truth. So in the Genesis story, the truth comes out: "We did what you told us not to do. We ate of the tree in the middle of the garden." This is a statement of fact, but two essential things are missing:

- a word to say that what was done was wrong
- a word of sorrow and regret for the damage caused

In fact, the story illustrates well what the sinner often does next—attempts to shift the blame: "I did it, but it was not my fault." The man blames the woman; the woman blames the snake; and the snake has no voice to pass on the blame! As we might say, it was a "snaky" thing to do—blame someone else. But this is what we do so often, and if we blame an object that cannot defend itself, so much the better. Nowadays computers get the blame for many human errors.

The God who has promised to uphold righteousness—to establish a world and a set of principles for behavior that are reliable—must now act for the good of all. God reveals how the result of sin is pain. Once the relationship of harmony is destroyed, it can only be rebuilt by judgment and love, justice and mercy. The story of the cross and the willing sacrifice of Christ is the proper conclusion of the story of the garden. In another garden, Gethsemane, Jesus, offers to fulfill the will of God, whatever the cost. God's rule that pain follows sin will be lived through and died for, so that we might know that love can overcome guilt, once we have admitted our sin, seen the truth, and accepted the victory of love that changes our life from sin to righteousness.

## Sin and Guilt

The account in the gospel of what happened after the cross illustrates for us the difference between sin and guilt. Sin is the action that causes pain. Guilt is the feeling we have when we know that we have done wrong. Guilt should lead to a request for forgiveness and a statement of sorrow. However, it can lead to violence against self and others. After the cross, the guilt of Peter first caused him to hide, but once he had met the risen Christ, he admitted his sin, and reestablished the relationship through the initiative of Christ's love. On the other hand, Judas Iscariot, in his guilt, did violence to himself because he could not believe that he could ever be forgiven. The authorities, also in their guilt, did violence to the disciples of Jesus. Guilt is an important step in our recovery from sin, but it is not the final step. It must lead to a confession of sin, a search for a new life, and a willingness to receive forgiveness.

Before we leave the issue of sin and move on to look closely at forgiveness, I want to help you clarify whether there is any difference between sin against God, sin against neighbor, and sin against self.

### Sin against God

We might say that sin against God includes the dangerous arrogance of saying

- that we can make up the rules by which we will live,
- that we can control nature,
- that we have no need of God,
- that we will use our faith in God when its suits us,
- that nothing about Jesus is true unless it fits into the scheme that our mind has created,
- that we will not acknowledge the generosity of God,
- and that God basically is not necessary for our existence.

We can also see that sin against God includes a failure to be involved in activities that would build up our relationship through prayer, worship, sacrament, and Bible study.

It is true that all these sins (of omission and commission) damage and hurt our relationship with God and the heart of God. Yet they also hurt us and our neighbors. If we start making up our own rules, we are certain to cause hurt to our neighbor, whose rights and needs we ignore. We will damage ourselves because we will become more and more isolated. We can therefore say that they are primarily sins against God, but that the consequences damage our neighbors and ourselves.

## Sin against Neighbor

The same principle follows for sins against our neighbors. Neighbor is the "other" in any relationship. Our closest family and our most distant enemy are both our neighbor in this sense. Sadly, we often hurt those closest to us even more than the stranger. Sins against neighbors include

- lack of respect for their differences
- demands on them to serve our needs
- isolation from them when we are troubled ourselves
- lust toward them when we use them as things for our pleasure
- failure to respond to their needs for emotional and practical love
- failure to thank those who assist us
- removal of them as competitors when we are desperate to be successful
- laughing at them or persecuting them so that we can feel superior

As you can see, there are lots of ways in which we fail to love our neighbors as ourselves.

Every time we sin against our neighbors, we are sinning against God, for we are breaking a fundamental rule that God has set down for living in this world—humanity is to live in harmony and mutual relationship with one another. Every sin against neighbor hurts us, for we are so bound together that sin rebounds from one side of the universe to the other. The fabric of human relationships is so essential and so tender that any damage is quickly felt in wider and wider circles. The failure of Adam and Eve to live in harmony with God and each other flows over until it reaches the conflict between Cain and Abel, and this ends in murder and death.

### Sin against Self

What are some examples of sin against self? We sin against ourselves

- when we neglect the body and soul, which is our gift from the Creator
- when we deny and suppress talents with which we are endowed
- when we refuse to open ourselves up to the love and care of others and God
- when we try to punish ourselves as a substitute for love

In general we could say that we sin against self every time we live for ourselves alone without any acknowledgment that we live for God and for others. It is obvious therefore that such sins affect our relationships with God and our neighbors. So all sin has effect even though we can identify who is primarily hurt by a sin.

## Forgiveness

Enough about sin. God does not want us to dwell on it, but to see it for what it is and for the harm it does and then to discover the means of healing and new living. There are three basic questions that people usually ask me at this point:

- How can we find forgiveness?
- Can we forget as well as forgive (and when is it appropriate and when is it not helpful to forget)?
- Can we go on being forgiven, even when we repeat sinful actions?

Let's look at each in turn.

### How Can We Find Forgiveness?

We find forgiveness when we realize that we are still loved despite the hurt that we have caused. Tentatively, and hardly believing that it could be true, we learn that we can trust God and others to forgive us. We know that we do not deserve such love, but that it comes to us out of a generous heart that is willing to absorb and accept the pain of the broken relationship. We discover that forgiveness is always a gift of love that others give to us. Such love is given freely, not because we can earn the right to be forgiven. Our part is to trust that we can be forgiven, and to be open to receive that forgiveness. To receive it, we need humility to make ourselves totally vulnerable by admitting our sinfulness. We have to accept responsibility for the hurt that we have caused to God, to our neighbor, and to ourselves. As we saw in the story of the garden of Eden, it is always hard for us to admit the fault. We want to shift the blame and to hide from the truth about ourselves. Often we cannot admit even to ourselves that we could act in such a damaging way. Yet we must do so if new life and good are to be resurrected out of the ashes of repentance. *Repentance* means a change of heart, facing in a new direction, and rejecting the false way of living. Along with repentance we need to find the words to say "sorry." To admit "I did it" is not the same as saying "I am very sorry that I did it." To say "sorry" is to show the other person that I know how much I have hurt the relationship, and I am full of sorrow and regret for that. It is impossible to receive forgiveness unless we admit with sorrow that we have sinned. Otherwise there is nothing recognizable to forgive. The hurt parties stay apart and become hardened to the pain caused by the sin. On the other hand, our sorrow shows that we do recognize that we can only trust that the generosity of the forgiver will be exercised on our behalf. Our sorrow shows that we will be humble enough to receive the forgiveness when it is offered.

## To Forgive and Forget

Only as we experience the generosity of forgiveness from God and from others can we learn to forgive those who hurt us. The experience of being in touch again with God and with our neighbor, of coming in from the cold of isolation, is such a source of wonder and joy that, when we are hurt, we too want to heal the isolation of the sinner. It is no wonder that Jesus taught his disciples to pray: *Forgive us our sins as we forgive those who sin against us.* To give and receive forgiveness is a sign that the rule of God reigns in our hearts. We are called upon to seek forgiveness and to offer forgiveness time and time again. Reconciliation is the aim of God. In the Maori language[1] the word used to translate "forgive" literally means "to pull up by the roots." It is a word borrowed from weeding a garden. Through forgiveness our wrongdoing is pulled up by the roots so that it cannot grow again. The place where the weed was "heals over," so that later there is no record of the fault. *To forgive and forget* is, in a sense, a

---

[1] This is one of the two official languages spoken in Aotearoa/New Zealand and is used in the prayer book of the Anglican Church there.

good description of the way that we should act toward one another. Saint Paul advises that "love does not keep a record of wrongs" (1 Cor. 13:5, TEV). Many people find it hard to grasp that God deletes any record of our sinfulness if we seek and receive forgiveness. Their experience of human forgiveness is so conditional that they imagine God must act in the same way—keeping a record of good and bad actions and seeing if we "deserve" to be forgiven. The actions of Jesus in expressing forgiveness in his life and in his death reveal the true picture of God's love toward us—it restores the relationship, it absorbs the hurts, it gives spiritual energy to us so that we can live in a new way. The cross and resurrection are the guarantee of this attitude of love in the Godhead.

Pause for a moment now to reflect on this and give thanks to God for such generosity.

There *are* times when it is not helpful to forget the circumstances in which we sinned. The sinner must be watchful of repeating the sin because the circumstances that led to it are the same. If our sin is one of violence or abuse, then we need to be aware of the circumstances that contributed to the sin. The issue of abuse has raised lots of questions about the "forgive and forget" principle. The abuser often demands forgiveness from the abused and by it tries to keep the abuse hidden. Forgiveness that comes too easily may mean that the reality of the hurt is kept secret. Forgiveness in this case can only be achieved when the abuse stops and both the abused and the abuser receive the counsel and support that results in true healing and new life. The beginning of such healing starts with the understanding by both that God's love and strength can reach them and restore them. Then, for the abuser, the full process of repentance and forgiveness must take place: accepting responsibility, admitting fault, expressing sorrow, receiving forgiveness, and restoring life. For the abused, a deep sense of the love of God will restore self-esteem, clarify whether there is any reason for guilty feelings, give a sense of cleansing from the experience, and help make forgiveness possible should the abuser repent.

## Repeating the Sin

The answer to the last of the three questions, Can we go on being forgiven when we repeat sinful actions? is yes, but...

God is aware, and so are people, that changes in our behavior take time to achieve. So we often have to seek forgiveness for a sin of the same type over and over. *But* we need to be aware that a new shape to life is always the aim of God's restoration for us. We often have to take stock of our whole pattern of life in order to avoid sinning in a certain way time and time again. God's love is offered to us seventy times seven, to use the biblical phrase, but the aim of the forgiveness is to allow us to leave the past behind and to move on to a new way of life. This will take discipline and dedication to God's way and a reliance on the power of the Holy Spirit. Those who experience the depth of God's forgiveness are no longer eager to sin. God's love revolutionizes our lives and gives us new goals and priorities to pursue.

## Receiving Forgiveness

What I have written has probably given you a lot to consider, both in your own life and in the way you react to others who have hurt you by their sins. Receiving forgiveness is like going to the doctor—you have to admit to yourself that you are ill and need help in making a recovery. You know that going to the doctor is good for your health, but it takes a certain amount of courage and trust to make and keep the appointment. At the doctor's office we need to give a full account of the disease and be subject to some helpful, probing questions to establish the causes as well as the symptoms of the disease. We know that recovery will take a little time, and that we might have to make changes to our life patterns. Yet we go to the doctor because our experience tells us that it is really worthwhile and that the doctor does everything in our best interests.

Without pushing the simile too far, God is our spiritual doctor, from whom we seek and receive forgiveness. God can meet us whenever we turn to seek the presence of God. Yet seeking and receiving forgiveness is a serious matter, and we would do well to set aside a time and place for such work. We may decide that it will be part of our regular soul time. If this is so, then find a set way by which you have an "order" for the dialogue with God. You will find some models of prayers at the end of the chapter. On the other hand, when we attend worship, we may want to use the opportunity of the set time of confession and absolution. In addition, some people want a "health check" type of occasion a few times a year, when a fuller examination of their lives can take place. To do this usually means seeking the assistance of a wise church leader/pastor/priest to share the review and to affirm the promise of God to forgive the sins of the repentant.

We can look at these different opportunities in turn.

### During Soul Time

First, we'll discuss the use of part of our regular soul time for repentance, confession, and receiving forgiveness. This is best when we have become aware of a sin and its consequences and want to tell God immediately how sorry we are and seek help in putting the matter right with God and perhaps also with others. In our awareness we take the following steps:

- We focus our minds on God's loving mercy.
- We tell God what has happened.
- We admit our responsibility
for our part in the sinful action.
- We express our sorrow and a willingness
to do as much as we can to put things right.
- We tell God how much we love God and
want to live a new life with the Holy Spirit's strength.

When we have done these things, we should keep silent and wait for our souls to hear the words of Christ—"Your sins are forgiven. Go in peace."

## During the Liturgy

The second opportunity is present at worship services that include a confession of sins, both personal and corporate, and a declaration of God's forgiveness, which some call absolution. One of the difficulties that the church has with the regular use of this part of the liturgy is that so many worshipers come unprepared for it. In the short time available when the opportunity is introduced, they cannot recall any sin that seems worth including, so they say the words without depth of meaning. We can come to the point when we feel we must say we're sorry in general for being human failures of one type or another. Because one person put it to me: "I seem to be expected to grovel before God." Because we are not really repentant about some particular thing, we do not feel forgiven about anything. Of course, it is different on those occasions when we go to worship with a heavy heart knowing full well that we have sinned. Then we are glad that the opportunity is there and probably want much more time spent on this part of the service. We are rather angry with those around us who seem so laid back about it all. As they sit impassively, we wait with thumping heart for the wonderful words—"Through the cross of Christ your sins are forgiven."

There are two ways of making the most of this regular opportunity to open our hearts to God in repentance and to open our ears to God's word of forgiveness. The first is to prepare before we go to worship or before the service begins, and to identify those things that we see as the sins (and there may only be a few) that we have committed individually or corporately. Some people write them down in shorthand form and tear the piece of paper up after the absolution. If we have already sought and found forgiveness from God, there is a second way of using the opportunity presented in church. This is to give thanks to God for the unconditional offer of forgiveness to us all and to ask for help in offering forgiveness to those who have hurt us. The Christian community believes that it is vitally important for this opportunity of confession and absolution to be there at every service for those who need it. This is especially true in those churches that have no regular opportunity for individuals to make their confessions to a listening pastor or priest.

**In the Presence of a Priest or Minister**

This leads to the third opportunity, when we know that a duly appointed person will be present to assist us as we express repentance and sorrow and seek forgiveness from God. The advantage of such a method is that you feel certain that God has heard your words of shame and sorrow for your sins. You are also affirmed by hearing the promise of God's forgiveness spoken by a human voice. Many have a great sense of relief and reassurance through using such an opportunity. Others think that no human should or could come between them and God. However, there is another side to this opportunity. The person alongside you as you make your confession to God, being properly trained and dedicated, can offer experienced advice as to what to do after you have received forgiveness. She or he can help you identify how you can put things right with your neighbor or seek help from a counselor to sort out some contributory factors to the sinful action. It is often helpful to discuss "What shall I do about it?" with another person, after receiving God's forgiveness. Such a person must be trained and ready to make a full commitment not to disclose what has been said in such circumstances. This level of trust is vital for the "external" person to be helpful in such a situation. It is especially important that the external person be aware of behavior that is damaging to the person making the confession or to those who have been hurt by the sin. The external person's main tasks however, are to be the listening ear and to speak the words of reassurance and affirmation that God does indeed forgive our sins. We sometimes need convincing of that fact.

## Forgiving Others

Most of this chapter has looked at the ways that we can seek and receive forgiveness. I want to end by looking at our obligation to forgive others and ways to achieve this. As I indicated earlier, we need to forgive others before we can realize how forgiveness comes from a generous heart that is ready to absorb the pain of the relationship broken through sin. Our forgiveness of others becomes possible when the spirit of God's love dwells in our hearts. Then it is natural for us to *want* to forgive. Yet we can only do so when we have helped the sinner to repent and express his or her sorrow. To make forgiveness appear easy is unhelpful because there is always a measure of pain that must be absorbed. On the other hand, to be hard-hearted about forgiveness is equally unhelpful, because we need to show the initiative of love to encourage repentance.

When someone approaches you to offer words that admit wrongdoing and express sorrow, then it is helpful to make signs and offer words of encouragement that you will listen and want to forgive. The person will want you to take the matter seriously and not laugh it off. Your ears will be open to listen intently. When you have heard and recognized the genuineness of their plea for forgiveness, then let your words in reply contain no "ifs" and "buts." Simply say, "I forgive you," and let the shalom between you be restored by an appropriate sign of being "in touch" again—an embrace, a clasp of the hands, and from a pastor/priest, a touch of blessing. After that, and maybe some tears together, sit down and talk about what you both will do to resurrect the new life in the power of the Spirit. You may be asked to help unravel some twisted strand in life's web. You may be asked to share in approaching someone else who has been hurt. Be careful not to accept blame for the situation if such blame does not lie with you. The one who asks your forgiveness must accept responsibility for her or his part in the sin or else there is nothing concrete that can be forgiven. In the end, you may find yourself encouraging the person to seek the forgiveness of God so that the whole of the circle can be "in touch" again to complete the shalom.

I bring this chapter to a conclusion with a series of prayers that you may find helpful for the various situations that I have covered in this chapter.

### A Prayer of Confession

*God, I know of your love in Christ Jesus, my Savior,*
*so I come to you to seek your forgiveness.*
*I confess to you that I have_____.*
*I admit my responsibility for these sins.*
*I am truly sorry and ask for your forgiveness.*
*Grant to me your words of absolution*
*and your strength to live a new life in the power of the Holy Spirit,*

*for I adore you, my gracious and generous God,*
*now and always. Amen.*

## A Prayer to Receive Forgiveness

*Dear God, open my heart to receive*
*your words of pardon and peace.*
*I hear Christ's words: "Your sins are forgiven."*
*My soul receives them with joy,*
   *and I long to keep your commandments.*
*You have taken away my guilt*
   *and set me free from the chains of my sins.*
*Help me to live this life of freedom in the discipline of discipleship.*
*Grant me your Spirit to renew my pattern of life.*
*Let me walk in your ways all the days of my life,*
*eager to serve you and ready to forgive those who hurt me.*
*So shall your kingdom come and your name be praised.*
*Alleluia. Amen.*

## A Prayer of Preparation for Confession

*God of mercy and judgment, help me to examine my life*
*so that it conforms with your will.*
*Show me my sins.*
*Make plain to me when and how*
*I have hurt my neighbor and you, my God.*
*Sharpen my conscience so that it signals my faults*
   *and measures my doings.*
*Make me aware of how I have failed to love you.*
*Make me sensitive to the pain I have caused others.*
*Give me the clarity to see myself,*
*and where I do not care enough*
*for the body and soul you have given me.*
*I wait in silence for your assurance of love*
*and your judgment on my words and actions.*
*Now I see that I did sin when I_____.*
*I will confess my sins to the Lord, I will not hide my wrongdoings,*
*for my God is compassionate and merciful,*
*always seeking the restoration of the sinner.*

## A Prayer to Help Me Forgive Others

*God of community, give me your spirit of love for others,*
*especially those who have caused me hurt through their sins.*
*Let anger not arise in my heart,*

*or a spirit of revenge or superiority.*
*Rather prepare my heart to forgive.*
*Let the way I act draw the sinner into faith so that I can forgive,*
*however hard the pain.*
*Let my ears be open to listen to the words of sorrow.*
*Let my mind be clear to see the causes of the sin.*
*Then shall I be able to help my sister/brother find true repentance,*
*seek full forgiveness, and find it,*
*not only from me, but from you,*
*our generous God,*
*for you absorb the pain*
*and by the cross assure us of reconciliation,*
*through the death and resurrection of your Son,*
*our Savior, Jesus Christ.*
*Amen.*

# 10
# Thanksgiving

### A Shout of Thanksgiving

One of the most common reactions that people show on being forgiven is to jump for joy and proclaim their thanks. Their thanksgiving is profuse. Something like these words flow from their lips:

Thank you. Thank you so much. It is so good
    of you to forgive me.
I do want to thank you from the bottom of my heart.
    Your generosity is overwhelming.
I don't deserve to be forgiven like this,
    so my thanks are all the greater.
I really am grateful for this chance to make a new beginning.

The writer of one of the psalms wanted to find the words to express heartfelt thanks to God not only for forgiveness, but also for the other gifts that God bestows on us all. If you would like to read all the verses, look up Psalm 103:1–12. The first five verses will give you a sample, which I reprint here:

Praise the Lord, O my soul,
    and all that is within me praise God's holy name.
Praise the Lord, O my soul,
    and forget not all that God has done for you,
The Lord forgives all your sins,
    and heals you of all your infirmities,
The Lord saves your life from the grave,
    and crowns you with love and mercy,

> The LORD fills your life with good things
> so that your youth is renewed like the eagle.[1]

Here the psalmist proclaims praise and thanks to God, giving the reasons for this thanksgiving. In every relationship, words and actions to show our thanks add to the existing level of love in the relationship. Thanksgiving affirms that neither person in the relationship takes the other for granted. Giving thanks is like a series of steps on a pathway that facilitates the climb to an ever higher level.

When we are young we sometimes feel that we are forced to say "thank you" to another person. The aim seems to be to hold us in a position of dependency or inferiority. It looks as if adults are in a powerful position to do all the giving, and the children are humbled by being on the receiving end, being the needy ones. "Now you must say thank you" becomes the commandment, and we dutifully (but not gladly!) obey. The thanks we give in such circumstances are an acknowledgment of the gift or kindness rather than a thanksgiving. When a young person is really grateful, then they show it with body actions as well as words. There is no need to prompt the correct response. It comes out naturally. There is mutual joy for the giver and the receiver. Both are delighted, and the thanksgiving is shown in the signs of love shared—a smother of kisses, an embrace or hugs, maybe a dance together.

## Cause for Thanksgiving

Of course, it is important, as we saw earlier, to acknowledge who God is and what God does. That is the foundation stone of our relationship with God. Thanksgiving is a further step on the pathway where we walk together in the relationship. The thoughts of dependency fade away in the mutuality of thanksgiving. We *want* to thank God so much that words, such as those of the psalmist, flow naturally from the springs of joy in our hearts. Like the psalmist, we will want to list those things that give us cause for thanksgiving.

First, we come to see what we previously acknowledged about God:

- God is the Creator of the world and loves it as an expression of God's being.
- God has entered into a relationship with humanity.
- God has sealed that relationship by participating in human life and death in the person of Jesus Christ.

---

[1] Translation from *A New Zealand Prayer Book / He Karakia Mihinare o Aotearoa*, (London: Collins, 1989), 315.

- God continues that relationship through the Holy Spirit, the Spirit of the risen Christ.
- God waits for the response of humanity in a partnership of activity to bring the whole world into renewed harmony and purpose.

All this applies *personally* to us through our relationship with God in Christ. We acknowledge the external situation, but we give thanks for the internal application of these facts to us personally:

- God is my Creator.
- I am made in the image of God.
- God has entered into a relationship with me.
- Jesus Christ lived and died for me.
- God's Holy Spirit dwells in my heart.
- The risen Christ shares the new life of eternity with me.
- God waits for me to be a partner of the kingdom of God.

The difference between acknowledgment and thanksgiving is made clear in the parallel situation between parent and child. A child is taught that parents love their children, and the child acknowledges that this is true. But when a parent says to a child with an embrace, "I love you dearly," then the child returns the sign of affection and accompanies it with the words, "I love you too, thanks for being *my* mom/dad."

Second, we give thanks when we recognize the generosity of God in a particular rather than general way. We may have occasion to thank God

- for a gift of healing
- for an answer to a prayer request
- for a vision of hope
- for some guidance or advice
- for strength to do a difficult task
- for an unexpected opportunity to use a talent
- for a teaching from the scriptures
- for a sense of comfort through the sacrament
- for a revelation of truth from a friend
- for a particular example of the beauty of the earth
- for a new awareness of God's love

Such actions follow the advice of the old hymn, "Count your many blessings, name them one by one. And it will surprise you, what the Lord hath done."

Third, we give thanks to God when there is a major step forward in our relationship with God. That may be our baptism, a development of faith, a deep experience of God's presence, the reception of the sacrament of holy communion, a call to new service, or the assurance of the life of resurrection. All these important advancements in our faith journey are a source of joy and thanksgiving to God. The recitation of the creed in worship can be a cry of thanksgiving as well as a pledge of faith. We give thanks for what we believe and for God's faith in us as well as our faith in God.

Lastly, we pour out our thanks to God when we know that we are forgiven by God. The deep sense of appreciation flows from a heart set free from guilt and from the fear that the broken relationship with God and our neighbor cannot be repaired. Such forgiveness comes from a generous God. We thank God for this outpouring of forgiveness and for our freedom to begin a new way of life. As the psalmist says, we feel that God has banished our sins to some distant place where they cannot oppress us again (Ps. 103:12). For that we want to thank God over and over again. Realizing that this generous love of God is made real for us in the cross of Christ, we want to give thanks personally to Jesus as our Savior. There is such depth of emotion in this thanksgiving that we want to weep over our sins and then weep again for joy as we hear Christ's words of forgiveness from the cross for our sins.

## Feelings in Thanksgiving

Those are the four main causes of thanksgiving for a Christian disciple. As we have seen, such thanksgiving is accompanied by feelings and emotion. I want to explore these feelings further. Ask yourself the question: How do you feel when someone expresses thanks to you?

Some people lap up words of thanksgiving. It gives them a wonderful buzz of feeling good about themselves. For them to be thanked is to feel appreciated and affirmed. They soak up thanksgiving and can never have enough of the feelings that it engenders. There are two possible reasons for this type of feeling. One is that the person is naturally delighted to be involved in an act of thanksgiving and will usually respond with great warmth to the person giving the thanks. The other reason is that the person receiving the thanks is starved for affirmation and, because of insecurity, longs for more and more words of thanks as a sign of being valued and needed. In this case, the warmth is not returned, and the person giving thanks feels the need to go on repeating the phrases to make the point—but it cannot be made because there is a bottomless pit of need for affirmation.

Other people are embarrassed when someone utters words of thanks to them. They stare at the floor and seem to shrink inside. They may blush. They would certainly find it difficult to embrace the person who said thank you. This embarrassment might arise because such people do not like the emotions that accompany the words of thanks. It might be because they are so unaccustomed to receiving thanks that they are not familiar with the experience and find it hard to know how to respond appropriately.

Other people seem to push away the words of thanks because they cannot believe that they deserve them. Such people struggle with feelings of inferiority that they could never live up to the image of kindness or goodness that others shape in their description of thanksgiving. They can almost be heard to say, "Do not thank me for things that I have done, which I cannot own for myself. I can never be that good. Do not thank me for it; otherwise I will feel guilty at not being worthy of your thanksgiving."

Other people refuse to listen to words of thanks because they fear it will make them dependent on the person expressing thanks and create an obligation for further generosity. You will hear them say, "Don't expect such generosity (kindness/forgiveness) again just because I helped you once." Life for these people seems to be a series of contracts and obligations. They think that one good deed must be repaid by another. The idea of generosity is foreign to such thinking.

Appropriate feelings of generosity and thanksgiving are spontaneous. They come from the heart without calculation or embarrassment. Most often, the person who is able to be truly generous is also the person who can give thanks most easily. It is important to explore one's motives in giving thanks to God and to others. Thanksgiving arises out of a sense of the generosity of God and of the "no strings attached" love of God. We do not give thanks out of a sense of duty or as a prelude to a request. We do not think that if we thank God enough, we will be treated as "deserving more favors." It seems the training we had when we were young shapes our attitudes toward thanksgiving, and when we are mature, we should find the courage to examine such attitudes carefully and correct them as necessary.

On the other hand, not to be able to express words of thanks at all is a condition from which we need to be freed. It can arise out of a wish to manipulate others. We can refuse to say thank you so that we never put ourselves in the "debt" of another person. In such circumstances my twisted mind tells me that I can make another person do more and more for me if she or he has to strive harder and harder to gain the "reward" of my words of thanks. To act like this robs another person of the dignity of being thanked. We hold emotional blackmail over them. Such manipulation can take the form of a statement such as "Don't tell me that you are grateful. Just show me by doing more for me." Such people usually have equal problems about generosity. They will withhold any gifts until they can exact more and more affection or work from another person. They may even use the double pressure of generosity/thanksgiving to wield power over another person. They might say, "When you really show your thanks to me for what I have done for you, I will do more for you." Such a statement confuses both the actions of generosity and the words of thanksgiving. Both have the aim of manipulation.

## Thanksgiving as Part of a Relationship

With this in mind, clarify for yourself the relationship that you know you have with God and see where true thanksgiving builds up that relationship. Remember, true thanksgiving

- comes from the heart spontaneously as you become aware of God's generosity
- helps you to realize how much God cares for all your needs
- keeps you from taking God's goodness toward you for granted
- expresses the love you feel for God as the source of all that is good and lifegiving for you
- gladdens the heart of God as the outpouring of gratitude from a creature to its Creator

Such thanksgiving is a central part of our total prayer life, as much as thanksgiving is a part of every true relationship. In that prayer time, set aside a period of time for thanksgiving. It is of course important that you leave space to hear God's words of thanks to you. That may be a new thought for some people! We may still struggle with the idea that God wants to express thanks to us as partners in the work of truth, justice, reconciliation, and peace. The scripture has these remarkable words from God to human beings: "Well done, thou good and faithful servant" (Mt. 25:21, KJV).

These are words of encouragement and thanks. Be sure to leave time in your prayers to listen to God's words of thanks to you:

Thank you for being involved with me in_____.
Thank you for your part in the healing of your friend.
Thank you for your prayers on behalf of the peacemakers.
Thank you for forgiving that "enemy"
    who has become your friend.
Thank you for your devotion and love for me
    in our soul times together.

Receive such words of thanks with the joy that these words always bring. Do not protest that you were only doing your duty, that you do not deserve it, or that it was God's spirit that made it possible for you to do what you did. We have already seen why such protests—though in a way they are true—would show that you still do not understand what thanksgiving is all about. Enjoy God's words of thanks and even congratulations! The more you learn to give and receive words of thanks, the more you will develop your spiritual health and make progress on your spiritual journey.

The use of thanksgiving as an integral part of soul time adds to your spiritual health because it strikes at the roots of the most insidious sin of all—being self-centered. I suspect that parents insist on making children say the words "thank you" in the hope that it will teach them not to be selfish. We can hardly think that everyone is there to make us the center of the world if we utter words that acknowledge that so much of life is "received" from the generosity of others. Through giving thanks, we become aware of what others do and provide for us. We realize that we are what we are because we are loved, but not because we are spoiled and pampered. In the end, we come to see that our very existence is made possible only out of the love and support we receive from others. Gratitude re-centers our being and makes us aware of how interdependent we are with other people. Giving thanks to God is a further way of putting our own existence in true perspective. We are loved, but not pampered. We are special, but not because we are spectacular. We are unique human beings, but such uniqueness is a gift from a generous God. Our hearts respond to such truth about ourselves with joyful thanksgiving. This enhances the relationship, but does not make us wrongly dependent on God. Our thanksgiving, if rendered spontaneously, delights God and affirms our own being as capable of giving thanks as well as receiving the gifts of life. There is no arrogance on our part toward God and no control of us by God in the act of mutual thanksgiving.

## An Antidote to Depression

From a relationship built up by thanksgiving, we are more capable of combating any feelings of depression and despondency. Mutual affirmation through the act of worship moves to a new height in mutual thanksgiving. Through it we have learned to listen to God's thanks to us and have moved away from any thoughts that we are not deserving of God's thanks. We therefore grow into people who have a more balanced assessment of ourselves. We know that words of thanks do not put us down by praising us beyond what we have done. Such false praise we know to be damaging and only a form of flattery. We know that thanksgiving is an essential part of our ability to appreciate what is of value to others in what we do in life. It is a key part of our measurement of what builds up others and is important for our life together. Such measurement is a necessary part of combating any feelings of depression. It stops our feeling that we are taken for granted and, at the same time, it helps us not to have such a pressure of achievement that anything less than one hundred percent is seen as imperfect.

Some depression is a clinical condition. Our bodies fail to produce the substances that engender a balance in our brains between realism and hope, between a sense of success and a sense of failure. The research into this physical condition that affects the brain is advancing rapidly, and it is wonderful to see the assistance that people can now receive through a balancing set of drugs. Obviously, there is also a close connection between the body and the soul, and I am sure that this connection works both ways. The practice of regular thanksgiving strengthens our ability to cope with our "down times," but some people will need additional help from their medical advisers and maybe a counselor. We will look at these issues again in the next two chapters.

## Giving Thanks to Others

From our experience of giving thanks to God, we can look again at the way that we give thanks to other people. In the busy, pressured lifestyle that is so prevalent among us today, we have cut out many niceties in life—and giving thanks to others is often one of them. We have even limited the vocabulary to a few short words and phrases:

"Thanks," "That's kind of you," or even, "You shouldn't have bothered, but thanks anyway." With the predominance of the telephone over written correspondence, we have let go of the art of expressing our thanks with careful consideration. When you have to write a thank-you letter, you have to identify the reasons that the gift or the experience delighted, pleased, or helped you. This is an important part of the thanksgiving. "Thanks for having us 'round" is hardly an adequate way of expressing thanks for time together over a meal. However, it is often how we speak over the telephone, and it only becomes obvious that it is too little once it is expressed on paper. In writing we would identify what it was that made us so grateful. We would say that it was the gracious reception that we received from our hosts, the delicious food they prepared, the delight in the conversations, the joy at meeting other friends again, and what fun it was to see the younger members of the household.

So a key ingredient in our thanksgiving to another person is to identify the causes of the assistance or generosity or pleasure and the response that you had to such actions or words. Part of our thanks is transmitted in the way that we let another person know how their actions or words had a positive effect on us. Our words might begin with the sentence: "Because you did this for me, I felt…" As we saw earlier, the giving of thanks builds up a relationship. It helps both parties to see what is positive in the actions/words of the other. The words of thanks acknowledge with emotion what others have done for us and show why this is so. This will be taken into account when needs arise at a later date. If a person who was feeling depressed is greatly helped by being taken for a drive to the seaside and explains in her words of thanks that this is so, then the friend will probably be ready to offer to do the same again. Without the explanation there is no way of judging how helpful the experience has been. The bare words "Thank you very much" are often ambiguous. They might express deeply felt thanks, or they might be a polite way of saying, "Thanks, but no thanks."

When it comes to giving thanks, it is important that we show honesty in generosity and in thanksgiving. Thanksgiving builds up a relationship to a point where both parties feel that the expression of thanks is exactly that and not flattery or false words of encouragement. We should reach a point where we can say, "Thank you" for some things that have been of help and, "No thank you" for other things that have not helped the situation. The relationship should be strong enough for such honesty. Without the truth we undermine the value of thanksgiving, because we suspect that if one part is false, then the other parts may also be untrue. It is important that we are told through honest thanksgiving what is of value and what is not valued. If we also add the reasons, then it is obvious that the words of thanks are about the value of the gifts rather than simply about the giver. To say, "No thank you" for something that was not helpful is not the same as saying to the giver: "I think you are worthless." We must find the words to thank the giver for wanting to assist us, the right words to show gratitude for what is of benefit, and to decline to receive what is not. Too often thanksgiving is reduced to affirmation. We give thanks to the giver as a sign that we want to please him rather than because what he has given to us is helpful. So the giver may go on giving us gifts that we really do not want or need, either to receive the affirmation of thanks or because he genuinely thinks that we find the gifts to be of value. Such confusion is destructive to the relationship. When we look at it this way we can see that honesty and graciousness are both important to our relationships. Such honesty should be a mark of our relationship with God as well. We may reach a point when we say to God, "Please do not give me any more opportunities for work for you. I am overloaded already." We might even find that we amend what we ask for in prayer when we realize that the answer is not something for which we could give genuine thanks to God. That type of honesty is necessary to a growing relationship.

## Receiving Thanks from Others

Now that we have learned more about how to express our thanks to others and to God, we should take a brief look at how good we are at receiving thanks from others. As we have noted, some people find it hard to be full of grace in receiving thanks and much prefer to be the giver. They may quote the scriptural verse: "It is more blessed to give than to receive" (Acts 20:35). Yet if no one receives, there is no point in giving! Gracious people know the joy of receiving or of giving, depending on which is appropriate to the situation. When we have received, we will overcome any feelings of inadequacy or dependence. We will not be open to manipulation. We will find the right words to thank the person and make clear to them the pleasure that their gift has given.

This mutual interchange of generosity and genuine thanksgiving is important for us all to develop. It enhances our spiritual health. Through such interchanges with other people, we can become agents of the Spirit of God. A generous spirit in us is always the result of the

Spirit's activity in our hearts. It overturns our selfishness and helps us reach out to others to respond to their proper needs. A gracious ability to render thanks is also the work of the Holy Spirit. In overturning our selfishness it prevents our taking for granted what others do for us. Both build up our humility as we acknowledge the interdependence by which we live. The practice of thanksgiving is a spiritual activity in which we are engaged through the power of God's Spirit. This gift of the Spirit comes through prayer and through the reception of the sacrament of holy communion.

## The Eucharist as Thanksgiving

The liturgy of the holy communion is often called the *eucharist*, a transliteration of the Greek word meaning to give thanks. The heart of all worship is the offering of God's love to us in a variety of ways and of our response to God in words of thanksgiving and praise and in deeds of service. In the eucharist God gives us the assurance of that love through the words of scripture, through their application in the sermon, through the petitions of our prayers, through the sharing of the peace between God and us and between us and our neighbor, through the remembrance of Christ's offering on the cross, and through the reception of the sacramental bread and wine in communion with the risen Lord. To all this our response is one of praise and thanksgiving. We learn to receive and to know how this reception of God's loving-kindness affects our lives. It brings delight; it brings guidance; it brings strength; it brings a sense of wisdom and justice in a distorted world; it brings a sense of wholeness and being in touch with God and neighbor—our true shalom.

Receiving the tangible sacrament of bread and wine gives us cause for thanksgiving, because it meets us in a physical as well as a spiritual way. It speaks to us of our daily bread as well as the heavenly bread of eternal life. When the time comes to offer prayer, to declare that, for us, this bread and wine will be the sacrament of the risen Lord, the theme is one of thanksgiving.

*Let us give thanks to God.*
  *It is right to offer thanks and praise.*

Such thanksgiving is for all of God's gifts to us:

- for the life in creation as well as the life in Christ;

- for the Holy Spirit's presence and power both in the sacrament of the body and blood of Christ and in the body of Christ who are the community of the faithful;

- for the past and for the future as we serve Christ and neighbor with the strength that we have received in this sacrament.

Thanksgiving and remembrance are intertwined in such liturgies, because one prompts the other. As we remember, so we give thanks. As we give thanks, we are more aware of what God has done and is doing for us. The events of Christ's life are the source of our hope and forgiveness. His baptism, his ministry to others, his words of revelation, his suffering and death, his resurrection and ascension, his bestowal of the Holy Spirit, and his everlasting presence are remembered for their contribution to our salvation. As we remember, we give thanks and apply Christ's saving work to our own lives. The transformed life becomes part of the offering of thanksgiving that we make to God. What we say with our lips, we show forth in our lives, and live out in service to God our words of thanksgiving. In some liturgies the final words of the service before the dismissal are "Thanks be to God." In another liturgy the prayer is for God to accept our thanks and praise:

> *Accept, O God, our sacrifice of praise.*
> **Amen.**
> *Accept our thanks for all you have done.*
> *Our hands were empty, and you filled them.*[2]

This note of thanksgiving should run through all our worship, whether corporate or personal, and you might like to use the phrase "Thanks be to God, I go to serve you" as one of your ways of ending your soul time. It will be a sign of gratitude and love and an offering of your life to fulfill what you have sought and prayed for.

## Causes for Thanksgiving

I would like to end this chapter with a practical exercise to make our thanksgiving more real and honest than I suspect is often the case. When we were looking, in the last chapter, at the best ways of finding full forgiveness, I suggested that you list the particular sins and some of the contributory factors and make them the basis of your prayer. The same realism needs to be applied to our prayers of thanksgiving to God, so I suggest again that you make a list. This time it will be of those things for which you want to thank God. Make it as definite as possible. It will, of course, contain such profound reasons for thanksgiving as our very existence—our lives. It may also contain such gifts as our ability to read this page, our food for today, and the

---

[2] *A New Zealand Prayer Book/He Karakia Mihinare o Aotearoa*, 490.

love we receive from God and from those close to us. Other causes for thanksgiving may include our delight at hearing a piece of music, receiving an unexpected letter or telephone call, having a dream of guidance or warning, being given the Spirit's advice or restraint about some issue that troubles or excites us, seeing the truth in a verse or passage of scripture, feeling the presence of Christ in the breaking of the bread, being guided to say the right words in a tough situation, and being able to "love a neighbor."

Our thanksgiving will also contain words of more spontaneous appreciation of God:

Thank you for becoming one with us in Christ Jesus.
Thank you for his cross and resurrection.
Thank you for the word he spoke to us in Holy Scripture.
Thank you for the beauty of creation.
Thank you for the gifts of the Spirit.
Thank you for the promise to be our Shepherd
   in the darkness of death.
Thank you for the hope of eternal life in your presence.
God, thank you for just loving me—always.

I have added all these examples so that your mind can focus on the things that *you* see as God's special gifts to you, for which you want to express your thanks and praise to God. When you have identified the clear causes for thanksgiving in your mind, or on paper in your list, then you might like to use this prayer.

## A Prayer of Thanksgiving

*O my God, give me a thankful heart so that I might be able*
*to express to you my deepest thanks for all your goodness to me.*
*I especially want to thank you for_____.*
*I sometimes find it hard not to take the basics of life for granted,*
*but now I see the importance of thanksgiving—to you and to me.*
*I want to praise and thank you like the psalmist.*
*I want to shout and jump for joy and say:*
   *Thanks be to you, O my God!*
*I want to celebrate your love with thankfulness.*
*Help me now to wait for your words of thanks to me.*
*. . .*
*I want to show my delight in our relationship with this song of*
   *thanksgiving:*
   *It is good to give thanks to the LORD,*

*to sing praise to your name O Most High;*
*to tell of your love in the morning,*
*and of your faithfulness during the night,*
*on the ten-stringed lyre and the lute,*
*with the tuneful sound of the harp.*
*For you, LORD, make me glad by your deeds.*
*I shout for joy at the works of your hands.*[3]

*Thanks be to you, my God. Amen.*
*Amen. I go to serve you.*

---

[3]Psalm 92:1–4 in the translation used for *A New Zealand Prayer Book/He Karakia Mihinare o Aotearoa.*

# 11
# The Withdrawal of God

I trust that your reading so far has helped you to journey deeper and deeper into a relationship with God and that your learning has helped you to such maturity that you can face your imperfections as well as your gifts. Maybe this book has excited you and given you a more positive outlook on your understanding of God and of yourself. It might then seem strange to you to see the title of this chapter, "The Withdrawal of God."

I feel the need to include it for two major reasons. First, because there is enough experience from those deeply engaged in the spiritual pilgrimage to confirm that most people have periods when it appears to them that God has withdrawn from the relationship. The second reason is because the experience of doubt is even more widespread and is often confused with the experience of the withdrawal of God. I will look at these reasons in that order.

## Recognizing the "Dark Night"

The experience of the withdrawal of God is well described by a spiritual father of this century in these words:

> On the road you have to learn how to wait.
> You have to experience your poverty,
> you have to accept the dark night,
> or the fog unexpectedly rising on occasion blotting out the sun.[1]

---
[1] Carlo Carretto, *I Sought and I Found: My Experience of God and the Church* (London: Darton, Longman, and Todd, 1984), 62.

This experience of the "dark night" comes to many people at various times in their spiritual journey. Surprisingly, it can come just after a wonderful experience of the closeness of God's presence. Christians have described to me how they have made a retreat and experienced some great truth about God and themselves, only to be thrown overboard into the depths of confusion shortly afterward. What had seemed to be so real became so distant. The closeness of God was followed by the withdrawal of God, and they wondered why.

Father Carretto's words help us to find the best possible explanation and the way to make the most of this experience. Read them through again and see if you can catch the depth of his perception of the truth. Two words stand out for me and strike a chord with my own experience. They are "wait" and "accept."

**Waiting**

All of life seems to be lived in such a hurry that we find it hard to wait. We are so eager to reach our destination. Our cars travel faster and faster, and our planes fly at great speed to try to beat the time zone changes. Humanity seems to have a terrible urge for speed. Some people live their lives in such a hurry that they appear to miss most of the best experiences. Children want to become adults as quickly as they can. Adults want to get ahead of others in the competitive world. Road rage overtakes those who want to overtake everyone else. We find it hard to wait.

In our spiritual lives we have a strong desire to reach the final stage of the relationship with God when everything will be perfect. Maybe you have even hurried through the reading of this book to see where it ends! The spiritual journey is not like that in this life. It is better described as a series of circles, and each time we repeat the circle, we understand God and ourselves all the better. So God insists that we "wait." We are to take time to consider each step. We are to wait so that we can consolidate the gains before we rush on to the next experience. The withdrawal of God allows us—even forces us—to go over the ground again. It gives us the opportunity to note well what we have learned. It provides a further chance to ask questions about our great experiences and to see what is important and what can be left behind. In our waiting periods we can also build up our energies to tackle the hurdles that are before us. So God withdraws in order to encourage us to wait, to take things at a more reasonable pace, to rest and resample the delights of the past. Waiting allows us to savor again the experiences of the recent events in our relationship with God.

Once we realize that the "withdrawal" by God is in our best interests, we will learn to use it positively. It is only when we are tempted to think that our faith to date has been in vain, and that God has left us for good, that we panic. "For good" in these circumstances can take on a positive rather than a negative connotation. In our positive acceptance of this waiting period we can use our recall of memory. We can bring the past into the present and let it sink deeply into our consciousness. Students of every age group find it important in a course of study to have a revision time. This is a time to catch the vision of the whole of the subject matter and a time to fit each piece of learning into the total picture. Only when we are "re-visioned" are we ready to proceed to the next major step in our learning. The same principle holds true in our relationship with God. Father Carretto is right. "On the road, you have to learn how to wait."

## Accepting

The second piece of wisdom in the quotation comes in the words "to accept." We speak of the "search for God," but in another sense we are the receivers rather than the finders in our relationship with God. The record of the coming of Jesus Christ is about God's initiative in revelation. "You came to us before we came to you"[2] is an important truth to learn about God. We can become so heady with excitement in our finding God that we sometimes fall into the trap of thinking that the relationship rests on our faith. We begin to think that we do the finding. Father Carretto points out that we need help to accept that the opposite is true, and God has to withdraw to make this possible. At that point, we experience our "poverty"—how little we know and how tender is our faith. We are brought back to reality if we accept the dark night. In the night we know what darkness is, and take stock of our need for light. In the "night" of illness we become aware again of our mortality. In the night we have to face our fears again with realism and overcome them in God's strength. In the night we have to rest our bodies so that they are prepared for the work of the new day. In the dark of night we realize how tiny we are in the vastness of the universe, whose farthest star lends its light in witness to the Creator.

---

[2] *A New Zealand Prayer Book/He Karakia Mihinare o Aotearoa* (London: Collins, 1989), 481.

Such learning can only be ours if we "accept" the night. If we try and pretend it is day, we will miss the sign. If we panic in the night, the darkness will close in on us. If we accept the night, this type of prayer becomes appropriate:

*In darkness and in light,*
*in trouble and in joy,*
*help us, heavenly Father,*
*to trust your love,*
*to serve your purpose,*
*and to praise your name,*
*through Jesus Christ our Lord. Amen.*[3]

## Lost in Fog

Father Carretto writes not only of the night, but of the fog, which unexpectedly obscures the sun. Those of us who have an experience of fog know that it is much more troublesome—even dangerous—than the darkness of night. We can adjust to the night if we accept its conditions. The night is an expected event, and this makes it easier to cope with the night. On the other hand, fog is unexpected. It obscures the route and blots out the familiar landmarks. There are times too in our spiritual pilgrimage when our experience of God is clouded with "fog." Nothing seems clear, the familiar landmarks are hidden, and we seem to have lost our sense of direction. These are times of testing when we have to look for the route with uncertain eyes. The question we have to face is whether we can say that God "withdraws" to allow such testing to be part of our spiritual journey. Is such testing for our own good, or is it the work of evil? With the hindsight of experience, I believe that testing is important for my spiritual growth. It is to be "accepted." It gives me the freedom to reexamine all the steps that I have taken along the way.

I remember having this sense of "fog" when I studied the Bible in a new way. I had the assistance of experts who had undertaken proper research and not just assumed certain outcomes. Up to that point, my own experience of the Bible had been positive, but I only saw it as a series of isolated words from God. I had no idea of the total picture. I could not explain what appeared to be "discrepancies." I would never have withstood the challenges of an intelligent inquirer. Yet the first onslaught of this teaching filled my head with "fog." I thought my

---

[3] An evening collect, from *A New Zealand Prayer Book/He Karakia Mihinare o Aotearoa* (London: Collins, 1989), 51.

faith would evaporate. In the end I realized that I would have to let go much of what I had thought before in order to enlarge and correct my knowledge. It was a difficult time, but it was essential for my development as a Christian. The key element in the survival of my faith during this period was the presence and support of experienced Christian guides. They understood what was happening in my mind and soul and encouraged me not to panic. They were realistic in knowing that I had to pass through real turmoil, but they gave me hope that a new shape to my Christian life and knowledge would emerge. As in times of real fog, a steady hand and a good guide familiar with the conditions will see you through.

## Christ's Testing

There is this element of testing in the record of Jesus' life in the gospels. The test is not there to "catch us out," but to help us prepare to face those situations that are inevitable in life. We cannot avoid them, so we need to prepare for them. Our times of "testing" make this possible. It is an internal struggle before we meet the external situation. Our best models for such testing are the experiences of Jesus in the desert and in the garden of Gethsemane. There are records of both in Luke's gospel.

The first experience is commonly known as the temptation of Jesus (Lk. 4:1–13). It is a time of struggle concerning the motives and methods that Jesus will use in his ministry. The call to this ministry had been the wonderful experience and affirmation received at his baptism in the Jordan. In his ministry Jesus was faced with the agonizing decision of how he would use his powers. Should he concentrate on the most obvious needs, like feeding the poor? Their plight was desperate, and their hunger was real. They needed as many loaves of bread as there were flat, round stones in the baked terrain in this desert. His testing made it clear that to concentrate on meeting the material needs of humanity would not satisfy their real hunger. They had souls as well as bodies. Both would need to be touched with divine power. There was a danger of Jesus' motives being misunderstood if he satisfied only the desire for an easy feed. Such a situation quickly arose during his ministry. We read of the feeding of "five thousand" hungry people with the scarce resources possessed by the disciples (Lk. 9:10–17). This is a turning point away from a public ministry of action in Luke's account. From then on Jesus concentrates on teaching and preparing his disciples for the clash with the authorities. Jesus tells his friends that he must suffer and die (Lk. 9:22). It is as if Jesus must make clear to them what he had learned in his time of testing. Jesus could bring salvation only through a cross and resurrection. This alone could bring the forgiveness and new life that our souls need in order to be satisfied.

Jesus' time of testing had to clarify motives that were to be used in his ministry. Did he, as Messiah, want to rule over the kingdoms of the world? If he did, force would be the course of action that seemed sensible and practical. Would not the ends justify the means? Violence would stamp out violence, and the hateful Roman Empire and its puppet kingdoms would be replaced by the kingdom of peace. Jesus' choice was the path of peace—with motives and means restricted to love.

In the temptations, the third point that was clarified was the means of demonstrating God's power. People would look for proof that Jesus was the Son of God, and they still do! Such "proof" could be demonstrated by a miraculous event. A safe jump from the very top of the temple during a festival would be ideal. Jesus rejected this. The situation that arose was the demand to come down from the cross (Lk. 23:35). But Jesus knew that God's existence and power can never be "proved." It is always a matter of faith backed by experience. You can never prove love—either in a divine or a human relationship. Once love needs to be proved it is not love, but control. Love always calls for a freely-given response.

We, like Jesus, have to withdraw from time to time to clarify our motives and the methods we will use in fulfilling our calling to be disciples of Christ and good neighbors to others. God is in such testing, but only by withdrawing to a distance. We must learn to work things through so that we come to such strong conclusions that we would be ready to die for them. The Spirit is there to uphold but not control. The scripture is there to discern but not dictate. In our testing we learn to reach mature decisions about how we are going to conduct our lives.

In the garden of Gethsemane, Jesus had to prepare himself for the inevitable trial with the secular and religious authorities (Lk. 22:39–46). His ministry had been building up to this clash. He had pushed the issues of the nature of God and the organization of religion right in the face of the temple hierarchy. He had refused to accept the popular role that the crowd shaped for a Messiah. The face-to-face encounter would take place soon. On that night Jesus knew that he must clarify whether he would go through with his motives and methods. Would he act by surrendering himself to the motive of love alone? Could he go on loving in the face of everyone's hatred? Was it the plan of God that he should offer his life for others and put himself in their hands to see if their instincts of love and justice would be greater than those of hatred and deceit? Was there not another way? Could he not do more for humanity by continuing his quiet ministry of love for individuals—healing, forgiving, training, and caring for them? He was so young.

This withdrawal of Jesus into the olive garden beside the country road to Bethany was necessary. Jesus had to be clear about how he would act, or there would be uncertainty at the crucial moment. The cross had to be embraced, not forced upon him. He had to be sure of the pathway of love. Jesus had to be convinced that this was God's will, which he would accept.

Like Jesus, we must come to accept for ourselves that the pathway we have to tread is one that God supports. We cannot reach this conclusion without withdrawal—both by our taking time out and by God's allowing us to own the decision. To rely too much on God would be to opt out of our role of accepting that this decision is both ours and God's. Here our relationship reaches a point of maturity. Father Carretto is correct. We have to "accept" the dark night so that the outcome is owned by us and God together. As we do so we will feel the comfort of God: "An angel from heaven appeared to him and gave him strength" (Lk. 22:43).

## Darkened by Our Doubts and Despair

The second cause of our feeling that God has withdrawn from the relationship is a different type of experience altogether. It arises out of our doubts and sometimes our despair. We do not feel that God has withdrawn from us. Rather, it is we who have drawn back from the relationship, because we are no longer sure that God exists. Such feelings are well described for us in this poem by contemporary Australian poet Pauline Young.

### Doubts

In the lonely darkness,
When sleep eludes me,
It comes to haunt.
This thought, this terror:
Supposing there is no one else
Who keeps the watch with me.
That He whom I imagine walks
Through light and darkened hours

> Is merely a portrait painted by my loneliness,
> That in reality
> He has slept these two thousand years.
> That the miracle is a myth,
> A legend and a lie.
> Soundless sobs, heart's hunger cry,
> Am I alone with my haunting fears
> And the silence of the stars?[4]

I think that it is true to say that we all have similar thoughts from time to time. It could be said that doubt is a contributor to faith. If we had no doubts, then we would not have to hold things in faith. Faith is necessary if we are to have the freedom to respond to or reject God's initiative of love. Doubt is part of the condition of being human. From time to time we doubt our own abilities. We doubt that others really love us. We doubt that the world is a positive place in which to live. On most occasions our faith responds to overcome such doubts. We know that we can never prove love, we can only have faith that it exists for us and can be renewed by us. Doubt, faith, and love are intertwined.

### Causes of Doubt

For a Christian, periods of doubt about the existence of God arise on a number of occasions:

1. when we feel that there is no answer to our prayers
2. when we are attacked by those "skeptics" who seem to have some good reasons to prove that there cannot be a God
3. when we are stressed by life's situations
4. when some human person has let us down, and God does not seem to fill the gap
5. when our best-laid plans come to nothing, and everything and everybody seem to be against us
6. when we are very tired, and our physical bodies are run down
7. when we are feeling very alone and isolated from friends and family
8. when we are angry and want to strike out at what is most important for us
9. when we suffer a severe loss

---

[4]"Doubts" © Pauline Young, in *An Anthology of Christian Verse*, ed. Francis Byrne, O.S.B. (Australia: Rigby Publishers, 1983).

In these situations our doubts seem stronger than our faith. As Pauline Young describes, we feel lonely, haunted, and fearful that all we thought was true is without reality, and everything is a lie. It is not that we feel self-assured and are so certain that we have no need of God. Rather we sob, and our hearts cry out in hunger for love. Instead of the night giving space for the stars to shine to the glory of God, it oppresses us with its silence, which adds to our feelings of isolation. Doubt gnaws at my stomach and leaves me with an ache of hunger that nothing material will satisfy for long.

Is it true that God has withdrawn, or have we buried our heads in our hands and blinded our eyes with tears? Are we like Mary Magdalene in the garden after the horrors of the crucifixion with her fears of grave robbers? We too can be so overcome with doubt and grief that we do not recognize the one who stands before us as the risen Lord. There are times when our eyes are so downcast that we do not see God. Yet there are other times when our doubts are even more profound and lasting. The foundation seems to have been shaken in the storm, and the whole house of faith seems full of cracks. "Is there a God?" we cry. "Does God care?" we moan. "Where is my faith?" We use this as a question to attack ourselves in our doubt. We may even reach such a low point that we repeat Jesus' cry on the cross: "My God, my God, why have you forsaken me?"(Mt. 27:46).

On my visit to an art gallery in Florence, I saw a picture which shed more light on this cry than all the sermons I have ever heard. The artist had painted a picture of Christ hanging in agony on the cross. The body was twisted, and the head was bowed. But there behind the cross, with arms outstretched to hold up the arms of the cross, was the figure of God the Father, and above the upright of the cross hovered the dove—the form of the Holy Spirit. The whole of the Trinity was there at the cross, its presence giving strength and support for the task that had to be done to bring back the faith of humanity in the forgiveness and righteousness of God. For a moment the Son could not see the Father, for Christ was struck down by the violence of man. "Hold thou thy cross before my closing eyes"[5] took on a whole new meaning for me as I saw the Father figure hold the weight of the cross in his arms. At the moment of our suffering God will be there "holding" us. Our faith may be blinded by our pain and tears. God has not withdrawn from us, though that is our fear when our faith weakens and doubt reigns supreme.

---

[5]The first line of the last verse of the hymn "Abide with Me," H. F. Lyte, *Chalice Hymnal* (St. Louis: Chalice Press, 1995), no. 636.

### Caring for Yourself in Doubt

Our best response in all the experiences I have listed is to treat ourselves with the kind of care and support that we would expect from God if at that moment our faith were strong enough then to believe that God was there. Be tender with yourself. Love yourself, not out of pity but out of a sense that you are worth loving. Draw deeply on the love of your friends. Ask them to minister to you. Let yourself be carried by others for a while. If you feel you are able to attend worship, go to be surrounded by the faith of the church rather than as a challenge to your own "not at the moment" faith. Try to avoid blaming yourself for losing your faith. Let it be a suspended judgment for the time being. If your prayers seem to have no one to hear them, just sit in reception-mode, resting quietly. Hold your hands out with palms upward and let go the tension of clasping your hands. When at home in your own space, play some favorite piece of music for yourself.

Unexpectedly, quietly, without much fuss, it is usual to find that you say to yourself: "An angel came and cared for me." The "angel" might be a spiritual experience from God or a human agent of God's love. That love transforms doubt into hope, and hope rekindles faith in due course. We may have to hold on to hope for some length of time. Hope will wait for the dawn to come, even when the sun is a long way from being visible in the sky. Hope lifts our eyes to gaze at the far horizon. Hope stops us from sinking into the pit of despair. It is true that hope is not the same as faith. Yet hope, like faith, is born out of love.

## Hope

When the agonies of deep doubt have been calmed, we can begin the road to recovery in the hope that what we have experienced of God in the past is true *for that time*. We recall such experiences, not to cast away doubt, but to affirm the reality of the experiences at the time they occurred. We do not compare the situation "then" and "now." Instead, we accept that they were real and a source of delight at the time. There are similarities here with the experience of grief. In grief we feel so alone that the memories of the shared experiences of the past seem very painful. At the first stages of grief, the contrasts between "now" and "then" cause sharp pain. A little later, when hope has begun to lift us out of the deepest grief, the memories of the past begin to be treasured for the delight that they gave us at the time. Our hope establishes that the past is not wiped out by the present. Hope allows us to savor the past as real for then and real again for us now as we remember. So it is with doubt and hope. By hope we are enabled to reestablish our memories of faith.

When we regain our faith in God, we may find that it is reborn and renewed, not just returned to what it was before. Our doubts will cause us to reexamine some of our attitudes and motives. In faith we learn to cast off some old, worn-out attitudes because there are new ones we have perceived that fit more appropriately into the current situation. For example, doubt may help us reexamine the way we expect God to answer our prayers. It may help us to throw off the magician-God whom we thought we could manipulate. Doubt may allow us to throw away the conception that God had a typewriter to record every word in the Bible—in English of course! Doubt may challenge our view of Jesus as a superman who never really had to struggle with the issues of being human. Doubt is hard, but it can be useful—even essential—to growth.

## Seeking Help

The period of doubt may last some time. During such a period we do need the support of friends and a spiritual guide. They are there to give you support and to prevent your being too hard on yourself. They are not there to argue for the presence of God. They are not there to drill you in the tenets of faith. Argument and finger-wagging are not ways to overcome doubt. Only love that gives birth to hope can help you travel on to the point where faith in its new shape returns. A wise spiritual guide will know the truth of such statements.

It is also possible in periods of doubt to suspend judgments about some things. There will be times in your life when you may be uncertain about some details of the structure of faith. For example, you may be certain that there is a God, but not sure that you can believe in angels. You may be certain of the resurrection, but not the details of the existence in eternity. A good spiritual guide will help you lay aside some issues for the moment in order that you may travel on in the relationship with God, allowing the future to unfold and the fuller picture to emerge.

In the last chapter I mentioned depression, which is a physical condition. Depressed people are often full of doubts—about their own abilities, about God, and about the future in general. In a depressed state we may find that our minds cannot find faith in a God of love. In such cases it is important that we have wise friends and pastors who can help us receive treatment for our depression. They will carry us with their prayers and their practical care. When we have recovered some of our equilibrium, we will be in a better position to regain the pathway to faith and to find the comforting presence of God for ourselves once more.

## Necessary for Growth

Having said all this, I hope that you can see that it is good to accept the understanding of the reality of God's withdrawal as a necessary, even if difficult, time to experience. It is not that God walks out on the relationship and leaves us stranded. It is a withdrawal, not desertion. It is a holding back to give us room to grow more fully. It is like a parent's training a child to ride a bicycle. The parent begins by sitting the child in the saddle and holding on to the seat and the handlebars. Gradually, as the child learns to pedal and the bicycle gains momentum, the parent draws the hand away from the seat. As the child begins to steer, the parent's hands are taken off the handlebars. Finally, running alongside, the parent lets go, and the child—with a few mishaps—learns to ride by him or herself. The parent is there watching, encouraging, loving, but the child, despite the protests, must learn and can only do this as the parent "withdraws."

Maybe it is like that with God. God may withdraw to encourage us to own our own abilities and to reenter the partnership with deeper faith, firmer vision, and purer love.

We have known our poverty, faced our doubts, waited in hope, and accepted the dark night so that the experience of the sun is fuller and richer than we have ever known before.

If you need them, here are some prayers to support you in times when God withdraws or doubt draws the curtain on God's presence.

## A Prayer When God Withdraws

*God, suddenly you have gone from me.*
*I had been so sure of you before—*
*and now you have vanished from my sight.*
*We were making such speedy progress,*
*and now everything has come to a halt.*
*I cannot understand, for we were doing so well together—you and I.*
*Help me to learn how to wait;*
*how to accept the dark night, and not to panic.*
*I find it hard to wait,*
*and I am no longer sure what I am waiting for.*
*Help me to look back to where I began with you*

*and to trace the pathway of our relationship.*
*Help me to leave behind what needs to be discarded*
*and then be ready to travel on.*
*I do not know where this will end,*
*but my hope is in you—*
*that even if I cannot see you,*
*you can still hear me,*
*O my God.*

## A Prayer in Times of Doubt

*God, I sought you, and I thought I had found you—*
*wonderful in goodness and everlasting in love.*
*But now I am not sure;*
*I am full of doubts and fears.*
*They devour my faith and destroy my confidence.*
*I am uncertain of the pathway and the goal.*
*I doubt myself, and worse still, O my God,*
*I doubt you.*
*If your Spirit still has any strength,*
*help me to love myself as you love me,*
*help me to be kind to myself as you have been kind to me.*
*Give me friends—wise and loving as you used to be for me.*
*Let them rekindle my hope, help me face my doubts,*
*and then we'll see.*
*Maybe I will regain faith's sight once more.*

# 12
# Using a Spiritual Director

In some ways the spiritual journey is a private matter. I feel that in this book we have been speaking to each other in a "one-on-one" situation. We have built up a relationship, especially if you have read through to this point! You have allowed me to guide and a challenge you in your dialogue with God, and I have appreciated the opportunity to be there for you. This has only been possible because we belong to a fellowship of those who are willing to "journey into God." Together we have been able to share prayer. Together we have been able to let the scriptures speak to us. Together we have waited upon the guidance of God. In the sacrament of holy communion it is the one Christ who has met us in broken bread and outpoured wine. We have been able to keep each other company on this journey into God because, although the dialogue with God is a personal matter, it is at the same time a "common" journey shared with millions of other followers of Jesus Christ. We can find encouragement from this fellowship of Christian people all learning to grow in discipleship. Therefore, we are never "lonely" on the journey. There is always the Spirit of God to be our Comforter and Guide. There is always the company of the fellowship of other Christians. There is always help at hand for those who need it and ask for it.

## Someone Near at Hand

Because I am an author at a distance, there may have been times during your reading of this book when you felt frustrated that I was not sitting beside you to answer your questions, give a further explanation, set out another example, or check whether your experience fitted into the picture I was outlining. That is why, from time to time, I have referred to a "wise friend" or a "pastor" or someone with whom you could share your thoughts." Because of such needs the church has appointed people under God who are trained and available to give spiritual guidance to those who ask for it. If such people are pastors or priests, they also have other functions in pastoral care and liturgy, in interpreting the word of God, and in giving leadership to a congregation. In the exercising of these roles, the work of spiritual direction has sometimes been overlooked. Because of the renewed interest in the last twenty years in the ministry of giving spiritual guidance, the number of training programs for those giving such guidance has increased. A variety of systems have developed for the giving of "spiritual direction" by those generally called "spiritual directors." Similar words can be used for what is not one defined system, but rather a cluster of system, with similar objectives. There is enough similarity between them for me to give the following general description of the terms used.

## Meeting with a Spiritual Director

A spiritual director is a Christian person experienced in the spiritual relationship with God through Jesus Christ. This individual has been trained how to listen while another person tells of his or her spiritual experience and seeks to help that person make progress in his or her spiritual journey.

To meet with a spiritual director provides an opportunity

- to articulate your experiences of God and self
- to express your feelings about these experiences
- to air issues that arise because of them
- to know that you are listened to with attention and respect
- to receive feedback
- to be challenged to be honest with yourself and God
- to maintain a balanced understanding of what is happening in your spiritual life
- to be supported in times of confusion
- to be encouraged to change in the light of new experience and fresh knowledge
- to use a framework of discipline to promote growth
- to measure your experiences against a wider set of experiences

As Kenneth Leech expresses succinctly in his new edition of *Soul Friend—Spiritual Direction in the Modern World*: "It is this process of spiritual maturing which is the purpose of Spiritual Direction."[1]

These are the sorts of aims that those of us offering spiritual direction have in mind when we undertake this ministry. We may not express them in a list on paper but in conversation and action, because the ministry is one of relationship—two people responding to each other and to God. Without being rigid we offer that ministry and when need arises may also add

- teaching a person how to pray
- interpreting the Bible
- outlining a theological understanding of God
- hearing a cry for forgiveness and repeating Christ's words of reconciliation
- identifying some personal issues that should be the subject of pastoral counseling
- recommending suitable books on prayer and the spiritual life
- advising on the opportunities to make a "retreat"
- affirming the person as valued by God
- marking the progress in the spiritual journey

Later I will try to distinguish the role of spiritual director from those of other people (or the same person in a different capacity) who offer other types of support to fellow Christians and inquirers. Now let me outline one or two of the variety of ways that a spiritual director usually goes about the task.

**Your Choice**

Spiritual directors will make it clear at the outset that they are available to be chosen or not chosen by you for this ministry. They know that the process will only work if you want it to happen. Therefore, you should have a preliminary meeting in which the spiritual director says what he or she might offer you and the methods that might be used. The initiative should always lie with you, and you should be comfortable with the type of person and the ministry. You will receive encouragement, I am sure, at the first meeting, but you should know that you are the one with the responsibility to make the choice about the relationship. Do not feel frightened (you may be a little nervous!), but rather be empowered to make your choice as a result of the preliminary meeting.

---

[1] Kenneth Leech, *Soul Friend—Spiritual Direction in the Modern World*, rev. ed. (London: Darton, Longman, and Todd, 1994), 33.

## Methods of Spiritual Direction

When you do make the choice of a spiritual director, there are two approaches to the task that are generally used. The first (often preferred for those just beginning) is to follow a program of themes to be covered in about a year. Such themes may come under the headings of

- developing a relationship with God
- discovering God, my neighbor, and myself
- in what ways do we experience God?
- what things are preventing the development of my relationships?
- how does my spiritual life make me a better neighbor?
- where does my worship with a congregation feed into my own spiritual journey?

The chapter headings in this book would make another program of themes that could be explored in the course of a first year. They touch on the basics of a relationship with God and how it affects our own growth as people and our relationship with our "neighbor." Another set of themes goes back to the first traditions of spiritual direction. It is the principle of the "three ways":

1. *Purgation*—starting a new direction, finding new priorities, rejecting all that hinders our relationship with God
2. *Illumination*—being enlightened with the gift of the Holy Spirit, seeing new truths, gaining a new perspective in life, understanding the mystical nature of God, gaining knowledge about the scriptures
3. *Union*—feeling closely aligned with God's will, enjoying the very presence of God, walking in step with the purposes of God for the whole world, knowing intuitively the actions of God in our lives and in the lives of others

The disciplines of prayer can form another set of themes to be explored in spiritual direction:

- prayer as entry into the presence of God
- prayer as mutual communication about all that is important to us and to God
- prayer as a sharing and empowering of our relationship with others
- prayer as part of our struggle for focused dedication to the will of God

- prayer as a time of confession and the receiving of forgiveness
- prayer as an act of thanksgiving
- prayer as support for the causes of the kingdom of God

All of the above will give you some idea of the possibilities of the ground that might be traveled during spiritual direction. These themes are like signposts that enable you to see where you have traveled and what progress you have made. They will also allow you to identify gaps and, at the end, to enjoy the completion of that particular set of "exercises."

The second approach used by some spiritual directors is entirely different. It is rooted in current experience rather than in accumulated wisdom. This approach uses the raw material of your own experience of God and of life as the means of reflecting on three basic questions:

1. What does this experience tell me about my relationship with God?
2. What does this experience tell me about my understanding and care of myself?
3. What does this experience tell me about my relationship with my neighbor?

The experiences themselves may arise from a verse of scripture, from an awareness of God or myself during a time of prayer, from a conversation with a neighbor, from a crisis in my life, from an awareness of the guidance of the Holy Spirit, from a sense of challenge in seeing a need, from a personal "encounter" with the risen Christ, from a struggle with the forces and powers of evil, or from an awareness of having sinned.

So, to our sessions of spiritual direction, we bring the story of our experiences. These are often graphic and so striking that we can reflect upon them and find where God is part of those experiences. The spiritual director will listen to our story and help us by prompting us with questions so that we see its significance and the issues that arise out of it for our spiritual journey. In the telling of the story, we will begin to identify those parts that are of importance and those parts that have no lasting significance. Once the experience is revealed and explored, the three questions can be addressed to it:

1. Where do I see God in it?
2. Where do I learn more about myself through it?

3. Where does it affect my neighbor?

Out of that will come a reason for adoration, affirmation, and amendment of life. These will probably lead on to a series of decisions and actions. You will find yourself saying

"I will not do that again,"
or "That is a good way to follow or act,"
or "I will do this or that as the next step."

**Prayer**

The final part of any session of spiritual direction is spent in prayer both by yourself and by your spiritual director. The prayer will give thanks, but it will also seek guidance and empowerment to do the things that have been identified as needing to be done. The time of spiritual direction should have allowed clarification of many matters, and, in prayer, we can share our key thoughts with God. It may be appropriate to have an opportunity for silence and reception of grace, guidance, and strength from God, and even for the use of Christ's assurance of forgiveness.

## Times

Whichever method is followed, it is likely that one hour or so will serve best as the opportunity for you and the spiritual director to be together. A much longer period of time cannot be easily sustained because of the degree of concentration required by both parties. Much less than an hour does not allow for a focused look in depth at all the issues involved. Restriction to an hour or so makes clear that after the session is over you will have tasks to be done. The work of growing to spiritual maturity is done by God and you. A spiritual director gives you the framework and support for the work, but cannot do it for you or instead of you. It is important for all involved to recognize that dependency ("I cannot do this without you") is not good for growth. There are times of crisis when you will need support and care to keep you on the road, but, generally, you must be prepared to enjoy the experiences and challenges that come from God and respond with your own decisions.

As far as the frequency of sessions is concerned, I would recommend that they be between four and six weeks apart. Anything shorter will not allow you to try things out, to make changes, to gain new experiences of God, and to take the steps that you decided should be done at the last meeting. Anything longer will mean that you do not have enough time within the hour to share all the experiences that you have had since the last meeting and then to reflect on their significance and what should be done about them.

I have heard of a useful alternative to this time sequence by which the two persons meet for a full day twice a year. This seems to suit some people who have learned the art of reflection for themselves and only need external help from time to time. This system of one day twice a year fits better with their cycle of discipline and a rather busy lifestyle. In this time sequence the particular role of the spiritual director is to measure progress and to maintain the enthusiasm for the personal routine of reflection on experience. The half-yearly opportunities will mark progress, identify confusion and gaps, affirm the reality of the experiences and their meaning, and set new goals for the next six months.

**Retreats**

In addition to having a regular time with a spiritual director, some people find it helpful to set time aside to make a "retreat." This seems an unusual word to describe what most of us find is a real opportunity to move forward in our relationship with God! A retreat is a time set aside from our usual occupations and surroundings in order to give priority to our relationship with God in dialogue, worship, and prayer. It allows for an extended period of silence, for reading and thinking, for focused prayer, for reception of the sacrament of holy communion, for the refreshment of the body through exercise, rest, and relaxation, and for the absorption of the beauty and wonder of God's creation in art, music, landscape, and sheer presence.

Like Jesus, we may want to use a time of retreat when we have some big decisions to make, when we have felt the burden and busyness of ministry to others, when we are wrestling with some part of the theology of God, when we want to pray for a particular person or group of people, or when we want to renew our progress in the spiritual life and take some new directions.

We can make a retreat on our own as long as we are clear about what we want to do and how we will focus on our relationship with God. We can make a retreat with others, led by an experienced "retreat conductor," who will provide springboards for God's revelation and conversation with us. Even when we are with others, we will still have much time to work on our own. We can make a retreat on a "one-on-one" basis with a chosen mentor, who might be our spiritual director. The practical essentials in finding a place for this retreat are that you need to "go apart" (change surroundings) and "create a space" with sufficient silence to have a two-way conversation with God. It is probably best to talk to your pastor/priest or your spiritual director about making a retreat and to find out from them what the opportunities are in your area.

## Not for Our Sake Alone

What I have said about spiritual direction and making a retreat may cause you to think that our progress in the spiritual life is very individualistic—that it is just between me and my God. The very opposite should be true. Our relationship with God always flows on and from our relationship with our neighbor. Our spiritual progress is not for our sake alone, but for the sake of the whole community of which we are part. The more I experience God, the more I can share this with my neighbor. As a Christian our journey will always be corporate as we contribute to the life and worship of a congregation. Our private prayer life will enrich our corporate prayer life. If we belong to a congregation where the service of holy communion allows us to partake of the sacrament regularly, we will want to be fed by God in this way as well as by the experiences of our soul time. One will "feed on" the other. The tradition of "solitary" religious people has always been balanced by a common fellowship and a common sacrament. Be careful not to cut yourself off from the life, witness, worship, and fellowship of a congregation. If you find it hard to relate to others, it is probably a sign that you are finding it hard to relate to yourself!

## Finding a Spiritual Director

Such issues would be just those that you would discuss with a spiritual director or, as Kenneth Leech phrased it, a "soul friend." You probably at this point want to know how you can find such a person to see if you and he/she could mutually benefit from sharing time together regularly. The first place to inquire about who might be available is through your own church. There may be a notice displayed there, or a secretary or leader may have a contact name and address. There are networks of people who have trained for spiritual direction, usually in an ecumenical group. The denomination and the gender of the people who offer this ministry do not matter as long as you retain the initiative in the choice and feel it is right for you. If there is no contact through your local church, then try approaching friends in different congregations. The practice is common enough in most countries for the news about who is available to be known in a wider circle. If you think that your local pastor would be a good person to do this work for you, ask him or her. However, it may be difficult to retain your freedom to say, "No, thank you," with pastors who like to take all responsibility for those committed to their care.

From one source or another you will probably hear who is considered "the best spiritual director in the district." To be honest, the likelihood that such a person will have space for you is very limited. However, what he or she will do for you is to recommend other suitable people. You will have tapped into the network and will have a number of names from which you can make a choice. Ask for a brief description of the person and his or her gifts. Remember that it is not a question of liking the person, but of working with them to allow your relationship with God to grow and develop.

## The Gifts in a Spiritual Director

You can expect spiritual directors to have lengthy experience and some formal training. They have to be equipped to minister to you in a particular way. They must be able to listen, to discern, to support, to guide, and to affirm, but *not* to control or dominate, to frighten, to lecture, or even to direct your experience. They must have patience to stand back and let you work things through with God for yourself. They should have the training to know when you should be referred to a counselor or even a medical doctor. This is why experience plus training is required. I understand that in most countries such training is offered both to those who are ordained and those who are "laypeople." It is clearly a duty that those who are ordained either offer the ministry of spiritual direction or know how to refer an inquiry to those who can meet such a need. A good pastor/priest will be aware of the principle of choice in this ministry and will feel no jealousy if one of the congregation chooses another person as spiritual director. Those ordained have a variety of responsibilities and obviously cannot spend all their time in spiritual direction unless the congregation has enabled them to "specialize." Those who dedicated themselves to the "religious life" over the centuries have provided a wonderful resource as spiritual directors to the church at large. Many such people in our generation are still able to give part of their time to this ministry.

## Pastoral Care and Counseling

Now it is time to recognize that in our spiritual journey there may be times of crisis and hurts from the past that place us in such turmoil that we need skilled help to sort out our problems. On these occasions we need in-depth pastoral care, and such healing enables us to continue our journey with God. We can liken it to having a broken leg on a journey. We may still be aware of where we are going and be conscious of God beside us, but we cannot move on until the leg is fully healed. In our spiritual life there are issues that so dominate our thoughts and energies that they must be attended to now for us to make progress again later. Such issues may be a breakdown in our personal relationships, a financial disaster, a crisis in the workplace, verbal or physical abuse, the death of someone close to us, physical exhaustion, depression, or other serious illness. These are just *some* examples that will help you recognize the condition. In such circumstances we need pastoral care and counseling and possibly medical attention.

If we have a good pastor or are in the process of spiritual direction, then we will be able to identify, with help, that we require skilled assistance and how this might be appropriately given. We will not expect the pastor/director to do the work so much as to help us find the best person to do it. The counselor or doctor will be fully trained and experienced in our condition and know how to give us the care we need. The pastor/director will encourage attention to the issue as a top priority and suggest ways that we can feel God supporting us while we are receiving human care. We may have to suspend our regular progress in the spiritual journey while this happens, but this does not mean that our relationship with God is unimportant. God will be very present in our times of trouble, and the Holy Spirit empowers our care and healing.

The counselor is there to help you accept that there are situations that have deeply wounded your psyche (and maybe your physical health) and that these can be overcome or integrated into a new pattern of life so that they no longer oppress you. Most of the terror they hold strikes you when you cannot see what is causing your present troubles. We are most afraid of what we cannot bring into our framework of continuous existence. It is the fear of something, rather than the thing itself, that causes the worst disturbance. A counselor can encourage us to reject something harmful—such as alcohol or drugs or temper—and replace it with a sense of deep love for the person we are, as that love is shown to us by God, by neighbor, and by self. A counselor can encourage us to integrate an experience—such as a loss of a job or a person close to us—into our future, giving us hope from God, from our deep resources within, and from our neighbor's care. A counselor can help us reconcile and make decisions about a broken relationship, so that the fear of being nothing can be overcome by the affirmation of God, of self, and of neighbor. Often while we are in the situation itself, we are stricken by the feeling that we cannot cope with life as affected by this situation. The counselor will help us reach the point when we can again say, "I *can* cope with this situation because…" If we need to see doctors, they may be able to give us medication or perform surgery that will enable the body to function more fully, so that we can pick up the threads of life with a positive outlook.

The spiritual director will assure us that our relationship with God will be strong enough for us to hold on to God and for God to hold on to us—even though there may be times of doubt and pain. Our pastor/priest will also give us care and keep us integrated with the Christian community, who will pray with us and for us as we receive the specialized help we need.

## A Team of Helpers

Pastoral care and spiritual direction will continue to be our supports for the long-term journey to maturity in our spiritual relationship with God. Along the way we may need additional special help from a medical doctor or a counselor. They will work as a team, but we should not confuse the roles that each has to take. It is the same God who empowers all. It is the same Spirit who sustains and guides. But there are a variety of skills to meet our various needs.

My encouragement to you is to use the various skills in a way that most helps you in your spiritual life. The goal is a mature and fuller relationship with God. Any persons who can assist you in reaching the goal are to be thanked for the ministry that they have to offer, and the glory given to God alone. If you need the help of a spiritual director, I pray that you will find one who is right for you and who is given the right graces by God. There is no doubt that those who have used their ministry witness to its blessing for them and for those whom they touch in life. It is not easy to challenge ourselves. It is hard to retain a balanced judgment about ourselves. There are times when we need their affirmation. At other times we need their assurance that God does forgive us when we repent. We need a person who can keep confidences, with whom to explore our doubts and our pains. Such a person can never replace God, but can stand and kneel with us as, with open hearts, we dialogue with God about what is most important for us in our lives. Spiritual direction is a wholesome ministry of service that many of you might do well to receive. It is now your choice as to how you will use it.

This prayer may help you as you make your choices.

### A Prayer for Guidance

*Listening God, in the dialogue you meet us with affirmation
and love.*
*God of the Word, you speak to us to reveal who you are and who
we are for you.*
*Guide us now as we seek to decide whether to find a spiritual
director to support us in our journey to maturity of faith and
love.*
*Make us humble enough to ask for help and strong enough to use it.*
*Give us a Christian fellowship that knows what gifts and skills their
members possess to support one another in love.*
*Give me clarity in my choices and perseverance to carry them
through.*

*Your Son, Jesus Christ, gave us an example of seeking the help of
his friends and of drawing apart to find space to focus in
prayer on the issues ahead.*
*Let the guidance of your Spirit direct me to choose the path
that brings me ever closer to you,
so that I may bring glory to your name and joy to my heart,
for you are my God, my companion, and my friend
now and to the day of your presence in heaven.
Amen.*

# Conclusion

### The Goal Is Heaven

In this book we have taken a first look at many of the basic issues in forming and maintaining a personal relationship with God. In the final chapter I have given advice as to how you might choose to continue the spiritual journey with a spiritual director. Sadly, then, it is time to draw to a conclusion this relationship between you, the reader, and me as author.

In our farewells let us wish each other "Godspeed" as we use our own soul times to continue our journey. The goal for us all is to attain what is known as "heaven"—the place/space where the relationship with God in love and purpose is fully matured. There our wills and the will of God are interwoven into a perfect fabric. There we feel so united with God that we have the confidence to enjoy each other's company to the full. There is mutual affirmation and we, as creature, find that words of praise flow readily on our lips to honor the Creator who gave us life and love.

We glimpse this heaven from time to time, and the foretaste makes us long for the final goal. This book will succeed in its purpose if it has stimulated its readers to undertake the journey and thirst for heaven. Along the way I hope that you have had some foretaste of the delights of the relationship with God and enough information and challenges to speed you on your way. Often it is misunderstandings that block our progress. I have attempted to bring these into the open and offer suggestions about how they might be corrected. As we still see "through a glass darkly," there will be times when we are confused. Prayer, books, and people can assist in clearing up these confusions.

I have given you examples of prayer throughout this book. I hope that by its end you will have grown in confidence to express your prayers in your own words. As far as books are concerned, I have added a Bibliography containing the details of some recent writings on the spiritual life. Most of these books should be available in a theological library near you. Some will be on the shelves of your local pastors and spiritual directors. Some books you will purchase to become your constant companions as guidebooks for the journey. Soul friends, pastors, spiritual directors, and counselors will be the people who will assist you with your questions and reflections. Above all, let the Holy Spirit be your Comforter and Guide as you move toward the goal of spiritual maturity:

Heaven —
   Hope fulfilled,
      Faith's path completed,
         God's welcoming embrace
            binds us in a unity of everlasting love.
   Myself revealed,
      God's face unveiled,
         in the company of friends.

   Christ's hands and mine intertwined in prayer
   "God's will be done."
         O pleasure of peace, O joy of justice,
            all our longings come to pass!

   Spirit-filled, soul-empowered,
      the child becomes the son,
         my life, my way, my end is God.

   Heaven beckons,
      and God waits…

It has been good to write this book because it has allowed me to refresh my relationship with God. I have learned again what must be done to persevere in progress toward the goal of heaven. May your soul time reflect its light and its joy, and may God go with you.

# Bibliography

Saint Augustine. *The Confessions.*
Byrne, Francis, O.S.B. *An Anthology of Christian Verse.* Australia: Rigby Publishers, 1982.
Carretto, Carlo. *I Sought and I Found—My Experience of God and the Church.* London: Darton, Longman, and Todd, 1984.
Leech, Kenneth. *Soul Friend—Spiritual Direction in the Modern World.* Rev. ed. London: Darton, Longman, and Todd, 1994.
*A New Zealand Prayer Book/He Karakia Mihinare o Aotearoa.* London: Collins, 1989.

## Books for Further Reading

Barry, William A. *Spiritual Direction and the Encounter with God—A Theological Inquiry.* New York: Paulist Press, 1992.
Bick, David. *Counseling and Spiritual Direction.* Edinburgh: Pentland Press, 1997.
Bryne, Lavinia, ed. *Traditions of Spiritual Guidance Collected from The Way.* Collegeville, Minn.: Liturgical Press, 1990.
Del Bene, Ron, and Mary Ann and Herb Montgomery. *Alone with God—a Guide for Personal Retreats.* Rev. ed. Nashville: Upper Room Books, 1992.
Fischer, Kathleen. *Women at the Well—Feminist Perspectives on Spiritual Direction.* New York: Paulist Press, 1988.
Guenther, Margaret. *Holy Listening—the Art of Spiritual Direction.* Cambridge: Cowley Publications, 1992.
Merton, Thomas. *Spiritual Direction and Meditation.* Collegeville, Minn.: Liturgical Press, 1960.
Peterson, Eugene. *The Contemplative Pastor—Returning to the Art of Spiritual Direction.* Grand Rapids: Eerdmans, 1989.
Thornton, Martin. *Spiritual Direction.* London: SPCK, 1984

# Index

Absolution 3, 67, 119–32
Abuse 126
Acceptance 148–50
Affirmation In., 3, 49–61, 136, 140, 169
Aids to soul time 12–13, 99–101
Anger, 3, 41, 69
Art 105, 107–8
Augustine, Saint 1–2
Baptism 12, 24–25, 27, 56, 136
Blame 121, 156
Carretto, Carlo  2, 147–50
Confession 3, 67, 119–32
Counselor 4, 45, 129, 170–71
Creation 5, 59–60, 95–96, 120
Culture  3, 105–17
Dark Night 3, 147–59
Depression 140, 157
Despair 81, 153
Discernment 73–74
Doubt 147, 153–59
Dreams 3, 8, 72
Eden, Garden of 106, 120–23
Eli 20–21, 30
Emotion 41, 43, 67–70, 78, 136
Eucharist 143–44
Failure 35, 57, 80, 119
Faith 79, 81, 94, 69, 97, 136, 149, 154–56, 158, 159
Fear 3, 33–47, 70
Foolishness 35–36
Forgiveness 3, 67, 107, 119–32, 133, 136
Francis, Saint 7, 60
Galilee, Sea of 77–78
Gender  3, 105–17
Generosity 42, 126, 137–38, 141–42
Gethsemane, Garden of 12, 22, 106, 122, 151–53
God as conservator 63–64

God as creator 63–64, 113, 120, 134–35
God as Father 31, 65, 108, 110, 112
God as guide 63, 66
God as judge 63, 67
God as lawgiver 63, 66
God as Lord 21, 63, 112
God as parent 29, 64–65, 108, 110
God as teacher 63, 65
God—concepts of 3, 26, 37, 44, 107–9
God—language for 3, 63–67, 105–17
God—presence of 5–10, 12–13, 22, 29, 44, 50
God's name 17
God, will of 3, 29–30, 55, 92, 94–96, 147–59, 173
God, withdrawal of 3, 147–59
Growth  14, 72, 158
Guilt 122
Healing 3, 27, 89, 91–104, 125, 135, 170
Heaven 3, 14, 173–74
Holy Places 6–7, 22, 107
Holy Spirit 7, 9, 11, 13–14, 21, 24–27, 29–31, 35–36, 39–40, 46, 50, 56–57, 60, 71–72, 75, 110, 113–17, 127, 130–131, 135, 142–43, 145, 152, 155, 161, 164–65, 170, 172, 174
Honesty 59, 141–42, 144
Hope 68, 70, 81, 85–89, 156–57, 159
Humanity 3, 40, 53, 56, 59–60, 64, 66–68, 123, 134, 148
Intellectual dishonesty 36–37
Intercession 3, 91–104
Isaiah 22–24

Jesus Christ 7–9, 13–14, 17, 19, 24–27, 28, 30–31, 35–40, 42–43, 46, 50–51, 56, 65, 67–71, 73, 77–79, 80, 82–83, 87–89, 92, 97–100, 102–3, 105, 108, 109–10, 112–16, 122, 125–26, 128, 130, 135–36, 143–145, 149–153, 155, 161–62
John the Baptist 24
Joy 68, 70–71
Leech, Kenneth 162, 168
Light 12–13, 26–28, 86, 106, 113, 149–50, 174
Liturgy of Intercession 102–4
Loss of control 37–38, 78, 80
Love 34, 40, 43, 45–46, 53, 68–70, 72, 78–79, 111, 119, 124, 126, 135–36, 152–54, 156
Miracle 95, 98–99
Money 54–55
Moses 15–18
Music 13, 54, 84–85, 156
Mystery 9, 33, 36, 113
Pain 120, 155
Panic 3, 78–80
Partnership 18, 21, 56, 74, 83, 92–93, 113
Pastor 3, 45, 129–30, 157, 162, 168–69
Paul, Saint 27–28
Peace 72, 78, 80, 91–92, 101
Personal Experience 5–10, 24, 28, 165
Philip, Saint 26
Pleasure 68
Prayers-concerning 84, 87, 91–104, 164–66
  For use 4, 11, 14, 18, 23, 31–32, 46–47, 53, 61, 70–71, 75, 87–89, 102–4, 106–7, 116–17, 130–32, 145–46, 150, 158–59, 172

Reflection 3, 22, 28, 167
Relationship 4, 19–47, 49, 53, 57, 59, 65, 119, 134–35, 138, 147–48, 153, 173–74
Repentance 3, 23, 119–32
Resurrection 95–97, 125, 136, 144
Retreat 163, 167–168
Revelation 3, 14, 16, 18, 26, 149
Righteousness 21–23, 121–22
Sacraments 3, 24–25, 28, 135–36, 143, 161, 168
Sacrifices 42, 50, 122, 144
Sadness 69–70
Samuel 20–21
Scriptures 3, 7–9, 19–32, 33, 35, 38, 52, 66–70, 77–79, 82–83, 85–87, 106, 108–9, 120–21, 133–35, 138, 150–53, 161, 163–65
Shame 39
Silence 3, 9, 166
Sin 3, 39, 119–32
Space 12
Spiritual depression 3, 147–59
Spiritual direction 3, 157, 161–74
Spiritual director 45, 161–74
Storms 77–89
Symbol 3, 51, 101–3, 107–8, 112
Taizé Community 85, 92
Testing 151–53
Thanksgiving 3, 51, 58, 75, 105, 106, 133–46
Three Ways 164
Time 11, 39, 53–54, 166–67
Unworthiness 3, 34, 137
Value 37, 39, 49, 54
Waiting 147–59
Worship 3, 49–61, 128, 156